Governance of Enterprise IT
based on COBIT®5

A management guide

Governance of Enterprise IT based on COBIT®5

A management guide

GEOFF HARMER

IT Governance Publishing

IT Governance Publishing
IT Governance Limited
Unit 3, Clive Court
Bartholomew's Walk
Cambridgeshire Business Park
Ely, Cambridgeshire
CB7 4EA
United Kingdom
www.itgovernance.co.uk

© Geoff Harmer 2013

First published in the United Kingdom in 2013
by IT Governance Publishing.

ISBN 978-1-84928-518-6

ABOUT THE AUTHOR

Geoff Harmer lives in the UK and is the Director of Maat Consulting Ltd, an independent provider of education and consultancy on best practices for IT governance and IT service management.

He has more than 30 years' experience in the IT industry and is a Chartered Engineer (CEng), Fellow of the British Computer Society (FBCS), Chartered Information Technology Professional (CITP) and is Certified in the Governance of Enterprise IT (CGEIT®).

After gaining a PhD in neutron physics at the University of Sheffield and conducting programming for scientific research in optical design at the University of Reading, he worked for Digital Equipment Company (DEC), a major computer vendor, for 13 years then moved to several consultancy houses specialising in IT strategy and IT service management for a further ten years before setting up Maat Consulting in 2004.

Since 2001, he has specialised in communicating and developing ideas and approaches around standards and frameworks for information technology through courses, workshops, public lectures, consultancy and writing blog columns. He regularly presents a wide range of courses that include certification exams – COBIT®, CGEIT®, ISO20000 and ITIL®.

He has been an Associate Lecturer in Technology with the UK Open University since 1999.

About the Author

As a physicist he is very interested in the linking of quantum mechanics to computing and so is currently studying Quantum Computation.

ACKNOWLEDGEMENTS

I first discovered COBIT® in 2004 when Gary Hardy ("father of COBIT®") visited the company I worked for in Reading, UK to discuss COBIT® and to explain that ISACA® was about to plan a COBIT® Foundation course. Unfortunately, as I was teaching an ITIL® course that day, I didn't get a chance to meet him, but I immediately downloaded COBIT®3 and was surprised to discover it had 34 processes compared to ITIL V2, which had just 10 processes. Gary had asked my manager, Sue Kilford, if someone who was an ITIL trainer with experience of Foundation course syllabi could attend a meeting at the University of Antwerp Management School (UAMS) to discuss the syllabus for a COBIT® Foundation Certification Course that ISACA® wished to create as an online course. I was delighted to be asked to attend that meeting.

At the two-day meeting, I met Erik Guldentops ("grandfather of COBIT®"), Gary Hardy ("father of COBIT®") and I was also introduced to Professor Wim van Grembergen, Chair of Information Systems Management at UAMS, a leading academic researcher in the field of IT governance whose textbooks written with Associate Professor Steven de Haes would later enlighten me. That meeting was when I became an IT governance enthusiast and I participated in further meetings to help define the COBIT® Foundation Certificate syllabus that came to life with an ISACA® online course and online exam in 2005.

I'd like to thank Sue Kilford for inviting me to get involved in COBIT® with its enthusiastic leaders Erik Guldentops and Gary Hardy, who have certainly educated me

vii

continually about COBIT®. Another COBIT® expert who has helped me considerably is Roger Southgate, who not only regularly presented about COBIT® at ISACA® meetings I attended in London, but also with Gary Hardy taught an Implementing COBIT® Certificate course that I attended at an ISACA® conference in London in 2006, enabling me to become an ISACA® accredited trainer for COBIT® in 2006 when classroom-based courses started.

Key to my success in the area of COBIT® training and consultancy has been Alan Calder, CEO of IT Governance Ltd, Ely, UK who in 2007 agreed to schedule COBIT® Foundation and COBIT® Implementation training courses using my company, Maat Consulting, and created opportunities for me to develop and teach other IT governance courses including CGEIT®. I also thank IT Governance staff Donna Garner for organising and managing training events for COBIT® and Elizabeth Quashie for setting up my accreditations with APMG for COBIT® and keeping me informed of the continually changing world of APMG/ISACA® qualifications.

I was delighted to be contacted by Vicki Utting of IT Governance Publishing (ITGP) with a request to write this textbook, and I thank her and her team for their advice, waiting a long time for me to complete it and for their editorial reviews. I would like to thank the following reviewers for their helpful suggestions: Brian Johnson, CA; Mark Thomas CGEIT, President, Escoute Consulting and S. D. Van Hove, Ed.D., FSM® SED-IT, CEO & Founder.

I thank my mother, Connie, and my late father, Frank, for their continual encouragement while supporting me at school and university and Nigel Kermode who persuaded me to become an IT professional instead of a physicist by

Acknowledgements

recruiting me to Digital Equipment Company (DEC) in 1982.

CONTENTS

Contents

Contents

INTRODUCTION

This book is a guide to the governance of enterprise IT (GEIT) and how this may be implemented using COBIT®5.

It covers the key concepts of COBIT 5 in order that IT service management and IT governance, risk and compliance (IT-GRC) practitioners can readily understand COBIT 5 and see how to drive implementation of GEIT using COBIT 5 and how process assessment is conducted.

The chapters in the book are:

Chapter 1: Governance – a discussion of the concepts of enterprise and governance and an explanation of the path from corporate governance to the governance of enterprise IT.

Chapter 2: Key Frameworks and Standards Supporting GEIT – a summary of the large number of frameworks and standards that COBIT 5 is built on.

Chapter 3: COBIT®: From Audit to GEIT – a brief discussion of the origin and history of COBIT.

Chapter 4: Overview of COBIT 5 – GEIT – the key concepts of COBIT 5, the 5 principles, 7 enablers and the goals cascade.

Chapter 5: The 7 Enablers of COBIT 5 – a detailed look at all the concepts and features of all 7 enablers.

Chapter 6: Domains and Processes – the structure of the 37 COBIT 5 processes.

Chapter 7: Implementation of GEIT with COBIT 5 – the approach to implementation of GEIT using COBIT 5 and an implementation lifecycle.

Chapter 8: COBIT 5 Process Assessment Model (PAM) – the approach to process assessment of COBIT 5 processes based on international Standard ISO/IEC 15504.

Chapter 9: COBIT 5 Resources – a discussion of the official ISACA® documentation and training courses and certifications for COBIT 5.

This book covers all parts of the syllabus for the COBIT 5 Foundation course, so it is a useful and readable guide for those planning to take the exam. It has practical advice and guidance too, so it is also a valuable resource for implementing the governance of enterprise IT and fully understanding how process assessment is conducted.

CHAPTER 1: GOVERNANCE

*'Corporate Governance began
In nineteen ninety-three
(which was rather late for me)
Between Robert Maxwell's fraud
And Cadbury's report to the LSE.'*

© 2009 Geoff Harmer
after *Annus Mirabilis*[1] by Philip Larkin (1922-1985)

This chapter discusses the development path that has led from the introduction of corporate governance to IT governance to the governance of enterprise IT (GEIT).

Enterprise and Governance

First let's clarify two terms we are going to use extensively in this book: *enterprise* and *governance*.

Enterprise (n) is the term used to describe a range of different organisations: a commercial business (often called a corporation) that may, or may not, be quoted on a stock exchange; a public sector organisation such as a local or national government department, or a not-for-profit organisation such as a non-governmental organisation (NGO) or a charity. Enterprise is a more generic term than business since business often implies there is commercial interest. Perhaps the term organisation could also have been used since it, too, covers the full range of different enterprises just discussed and the term organisation chart is

---

[1] Larkin, P. A. (1967), Annus Mirabilis, in *High Windows*, (new edition 1979), London, Faber and Faber.

commonly used in all types of enterprises[2]. However, enterprise has become the term frequently used in the 21st century when discussing governance of organisations: that is, enterprise governance.

Governance (n) is 'the action, manner or fact of governing; controlling or regulating influence or good order[3]'.

Clearly, governance applied to enterprises is expressing the view that directors (or top management) of enterprises are tasked with governing, controlling and regulating their enterprise using best practices. Shareholders who appoint directors, as well as citizens who elect governments, expect this to take place but in some enterprises this has not happened and legal actions have had to be taken against many directors and top management over the centuries. Imprisonment and huge fines was not the only answer; what was needed was advice and guidance through regulations that must be obeyed – that is, corporate governance codes.

Emergence of Governance Codes

It was following Robert Maxwell's death in 1990 that a £4 billion fraud at Maxwell Communication Corporation and Mirror Group Newspapers was revealed. Maxwell was both chairman and chief executive – now considered not ideal and segregation of duties for these two roles is now best practice. Other frauds in enterprises quoted on the London Stock Exchange (LSE) around this time were Bank of

---

[2] A senior IT manager from a major UK government department confirmed that enterprise is a better term than organisation since the large government department where he works is broken into a number of *organisations*, so the government department is an *enterprise*.

[3] The New Shorter Oxford Dictionary (1993), Oxford, Oxford University Press.

Credit and Commerce International (BCCI) in 1991 and Polly Peck in 1990. These enterprises are all known in the UK as corporations – a word that implies stock market quoted enterprises. Consequently in 1991, the LSE and the accountancy profession appointed Sir Adrian Cadbury to chair a committee to recommend a code of best practice for corporate governance. The resulting Cadbury Report: *Financial Aspects of Corporate Governance* (December 1992)[4] is often seen as the point at which formally defined corporate governance emerged. The Cadbury Report identified the key responsibilities of boards of directors to be setting strategy, providing leadership, supervising management and reporting to shareholders about board stewardship (i.e. properly running the corporation in a fiduciary, i.e. trustworthy, way that the shareholders requested and expected).

Barger (2004)[5], *see Figure 1.1*, explained corporate governance very succinctly, stating there are three parts: ownership, governance and management. She indicated that shareholders had ownership of a corporation and appointed directors to govern the corporation. The directors' duty was to protect the shareholders' investment in the corporation by working with management to develop a corporate strategy and by directing management to run the corporation. Management's job was 'to develop business capabilities' and 'run business operations'. The directors would also request the management to provide reports so

---

[4] Cadbury Report (1992), *Financial Aspects of Corporate Governance.*
[5] Barger, T. (2004) Corporate Governance – A Working Definition, *International Corporate Governance Meeting*, Hanoi: IFC/World Bank Corporate Governance Department.

they could monitor whether their management was meeting directives.

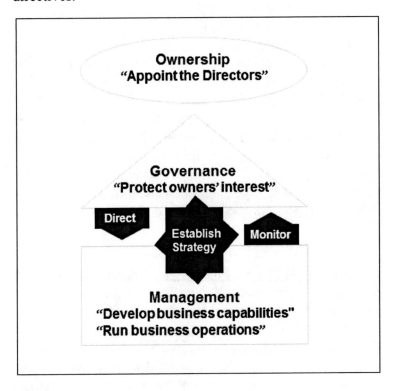

Figure 1.1 Corporate Governance (Based on Barger, 2004)

Corporate governance is now well established in the world, for example, all G-20 countries and, in total, more than 90 countries have their own corporate governance recommendations known as corporate governance codes (ECGI, 2013)[6].

---

[6] ECGI (2013) *www.ecgi.org/codes/all_codes.php.*

The International Federation of Accountants (IFAC, 2004)[7] used the term enterprise governance and indicated this includes two parts: Business Governance (i.e. performance) and Corporate Governance (i.e. conformance). Performance covers activities for value creation, resource utilisation and risk management. Conformance covers accountability and assurance. However, much earlier, Tricker, in his seminal textbook *Corporate Governance* – first written in 1984 when 'the term corporate governance was not then in use' (Tricker, 2008)[8] – indicated that corporate governance includes compliance (i.e. conformance) and performance. So enterprise governance means corporate governance. Interestingly, the Chartered Institute of Management Accountants (CIMA) who also used to say Enterprise Governance is made up of Corporate Governance and Business Governance has now removed both those terms and just talks about Enterprise Governance as performance and conformance (CIMA, 2010)[9].

When did IT Governance emerge?

As Weill and Ross, 2004[10], indicated in the preface to their seminal textbook, *IT Governance*, the point at which the importance of conducting IT Governance became clear is

---

[7] IFAC (2004) [online] Enterprise governance- getting the balance right, *www.ifac.org/sites/default/files/publications/files/enterprise-governance-gett-1.pdf* [accessed 30 Aug 2013].
[8] Tricker, R.I. (2008) *Corporate Governance: Principles, Policies and Practices,* Oxford, Oxford University Press.
[9] CIMA (2010) Enterprise governance – restoring boardroom leadership, [online], *www.cimaglobal.com/Documents/Thought_leadership_docs/Enterprise_governance.pdf,* [accessed 30 Aug 2013].
[10] Weill, P. & Ross, J.W. (2004) *IT Governance,* Boston. Harvard Business School Press.

not well defined like that of corporate governance but emerged over a period of years from multiple research studies and discussions between managers. As early as 1998-9 Weill with Michael Vitale at the Melbourne Business School conducted an exploratory study of IT governance. Much of the work on business and IT alignment (BITA) in the 1990s contributed to IT governance, too. The earliest I have been able to find the term IT governance was in an article on strategic alignment of business and IT by Henderson and Venkatraman in 1992 in Chapter 7 of the book *Transforming Organisations* (Kochan and Useem)[11].

IT governance took off as a discipline once the COBIT framework evolved from an IT audit to an IT governance framework with the release of COBIT®3.0 in 2000. COBIT was, and still is, widely adopted as the *de facto* framework to meet the IT governance requirements of Section 404 of the Sarbanes-Oxley Act of 2002. It is worth pointing out that COBIT recognised that IT governance was concerned with ensuring both conformance and performance, that is, compliance and value delivery to the business.

In Australia between 2003 and 2005, Standards Australia developed Australian Standard AS 8015-2005 for the Corporate Governance of Information and Communication Technology. This complemented the set of Australian Corporate Governance Standards – the first of which had been published in 2003. AS 8015 was fast-tracked into an ISO Standard as ISO/IEC 38500, *Corporate Governance of IT*, published in May 2008. Unlike the free, comprehensive

---

[11] Kochan, T. A. and Useem, M (1997) *Transforming Organisation*, New York, Oxford University Press Inc.

resources within the COBIT framework, ISO/IEC 38500 was a slim, 12-page, easy-to-understand Standard aimed at directors of businesses to guide them in their governance in the use of IT – however, it has to be purchased at around $100.

Clearly COBIT needed to take on board the ISO/IEC 38500 Standard and this was to happen with COBIT 5.

Now people are starting to discuss Enterprise Governance of IT rather than IT Governance; notably Wim Van Grembergen and Steven De Haes at the University of Antwerp Management School (UAMS). They have been long-term researchers for ISACA/ITGI and advocates of approaches to implementation of IT governance that have contributed much to the development of the COBIT framework. In their book *Enterprise Governance of Information Technology*[12], published in 2009, they begin by pointing out that Enterprise Governance of IT is a relatively new term and they go on to explain that because of the 'IT' in the naming of IT governance, discussion did not generally reach the boardrooms of organisations. Clearly the involvement of business is crucial and they indicate there has been a shift of emphasis (largely due to the publication of ISO/IEC 38500, I feel) to focus on business involvement, that is, Enterprise Governance of IT. As they put it, 'Enterprise Governance of IT is an integral part of corporate governance and addresses the definition and implementation of processes, structures and relational mechanisms in the organisation that enables both business and IT people to execute their responsibilities in support of

---

[12] Van Grembergen, W. & De Haes, S. (2009) *Enterprise Governance of Information Technology*, New York, Springer Science + Business Media LLC.

business/IT alignment and the creation of business value from IT-enabled investments.'

In 2009, ISACA created a new certificate called Certified in the Governance of Enterprise IT (CGEIT®) that is a person qualification based on passing an examination and having sufficient professional experience of the governance of enterprise IT. Notice that the term Governance of Enterprise IT (GEIT) is a rephrasing of Van Grembergen and De Haes' term 'Enterprise Governance of IT'. GEIT is now the conventional term for what earlier was, and still is, referred to as IT governance.

So from 2010, the COBIT 5 Task Force worked on COBIT®5 that was released in April 2012. It is aligned with ISO/IEC 38500 and it fully addresses the 'Governance of Enterprise IT'. That is the subject of this book.

CHAPTER 2: KEY FRAMEWORKS AND STANDARDS SUPPORTING GOVERNANCE OF ENTERPRISE IT

'The nice thing about standards is that you have so many to choose from. [13]

Andrew S Tannebaum (1981)
Computer Networks, 1st Edition, p. 168

In this chapter, under basic headings, many key frameworks and international standards that are the basis for COBIT 5ʹ are briefly discussed and footnote references are provided to sources of further information – mostly readily accessible on the Internet for free.

Governance of enterprise IT is concerned with both governance and management and requires a broad range of practices to be included. ISACA has always been very good at recognising such practices and has always used well-known frameworks and international standards as the basis for the development of COBIT. For example, COBIT®4.1 was quoted by ISACA as being based on more than 40 other frameworks and standards and COBIT 5 is claimed to be based on more than 80 frameworks and standards.

---

[13] In this chapter 33 standards and frameworks are briefly discussed.

IT Governance

As explained in *Chapter 1*, IT Governance is the original but still popular term for Governance of Enterprise IT (GEIT) and Corporate Governance of IT.

ISO/IEC 38500: 2008 Corporate Governance of Information Technology

An international Standard based on an Australian Standard, AS 8015-2005, that specifies the three activities to be conducted by board members and senior executives who are accountable and responsible for corporate governance of IT.

1. Evaluate
2. Direct
3. Monitor

The Standard also specifies the six key principles of corporate governance of IT:

1. Responsibility
2. Strategy
3. Acquisition
4. Performance
5. Conformance
6. Human Behaviour

ISACA has adopted the three activities Evaluate, Direct and Monitor of ISO/IEC 38500 and these are governance practices of each of the five processes in the Governance Domain of COBIT 5. These governance practices are titled:

- evaluate the governance system
- direct the governance system
- monitor the governance system.

However, the six key principles of ISO/IEC 38500 have not been formally adopted by COBIT 5, although COBIT 5 does support the adoption of these principles and explains how COBIT 5 guidance enables each of these principles[14].

Two standards related to ISO/IEC 38500 are under development by ISO TC/SC JTC1. Targeted for publication in 2016 is ISO/IEC 38501[15] Corporate Governance of IT Implementation Guide, and ISO/IEC 38502[16] Governance of IT – Framework and Model may be ready for publication in 2014.

IT Service Management

In this section the following will be discussed:

- ITIL 2011 Edition
- ISO/IEC 20000: 2011

IT Infrastructure Library (ITIL) 2011 Edition[17]

ITIL, which was first published in 1989, is almost certainly the most deployed framework in the world for IT. An indicator of the level of deployment is the fact that by the end of 2012 the number of people holding an ITIL Foundation Certificate exceeded two million and each month 20-25,000 people are passing the ITIL Foundation exam.

ITIL is concerned with best practices for the delivery of IT services to businesses and is based on three key areas:

---

[14] ISACA® (2012) COBIT®5: A Business Framework for the Governance and Management of Enterprise IT, Appendix E, pp. 57–60.
[15] *www.iso.org/iso/home/store/catalogue_tc/catalogue_detail.htm?csnumber=45263*
[16] *www.iso.org/iso/home/store/catalogue_tc/catalogue_detail.htm?csnumber=50962*
[17] *www.itil-officialsite.com/*

- Services – IT applications that support business processes and activities
- Processes – these processes are used to control and manage IT services
- Functions – organisational units in the IT department

ITIL 2011 Edition is service lifecycle based:

- Service Strategy
- Service Design
- Service Transition
- Service Operation
- Continual Service Improvement

ITIL has 26 processes (*Table 2.1*) and four functions (*Table 2.2*).

Table 2.1: ITIL Processes

Lifecycle Phase	ITIL Processes
Service Strategy	Strategy management for IT services
	Demand management
	Portfolio management
	Business relationship management
	Finance management for IT services
Service Design	Design coordination
	Service level management
	Service catalogue management

Table 2.1: ITIL Processes cont.

Lifecycle Phase	ITIL Processes
Service Design cont.	Availability management
	Capacity management
	Information security management
	Supplier management
	IT service continuity management
Service Transition	Transition planning and support
	Change management
	Release and deployment management
	Service asset and configuration management
	Knowledge management
	Service validation and testing
	Change evaluation
Service Operation	Incident management
	Request fulfilment
	Problem management
	Access management
	Event management
Continual Service Improvement	Seven-step service improvement process

Table 2.2: ITIL Functions

Functions
Service Desk
Technical Management
Application Management

IT Operations Management:
   • IT Operations Control
   • Facilities Management

ITIL is listed in the *COBIT 5: Enabling Processes* book as providing related guidance to 15 of the 37 COBIT 5 processes – *see Appendix A*.

ISO/IEC 20000: 2011 Information technology service management system

ISO/IEC 20000 was originally developed in 2000 as British Standard BS 15000 using ITIL V2 as its main source of ITSM practices. It was developed as the basis for certification of organisations for IT service management. To gain certification an organisation has to be externally audited for compliance with the Standard, which confirms that the organisation is using recognised ITSM practices for the delivery of IT service management. BS 15000 was internationalised as ISO/IEC 20000 in 2005. However, in 2011, it was upgraded to reflect developments in IT service management practices in the decade since BS 15000 was first introduced and the revision particularly took on board more fully the concepts of management systems that are formally used in other standards: in particular, ISO9000 (Quality) and ISO/IEC 27001 (Information security).

ISO/IEC 20000 describes a service management system (SMS) – *See Figure 2.1* – that must be in place in its entirety for an organisation to gain an ISO/IEC 20000 certificate[18]. Certification is reassessed every three years and surveillance audited at least annually in the interim period. More than 600 organisations in the world held the APM Group ISO/IEC 20000: 2011 certificate in September 2013.

---

[18] www.isoiec20000certification.com

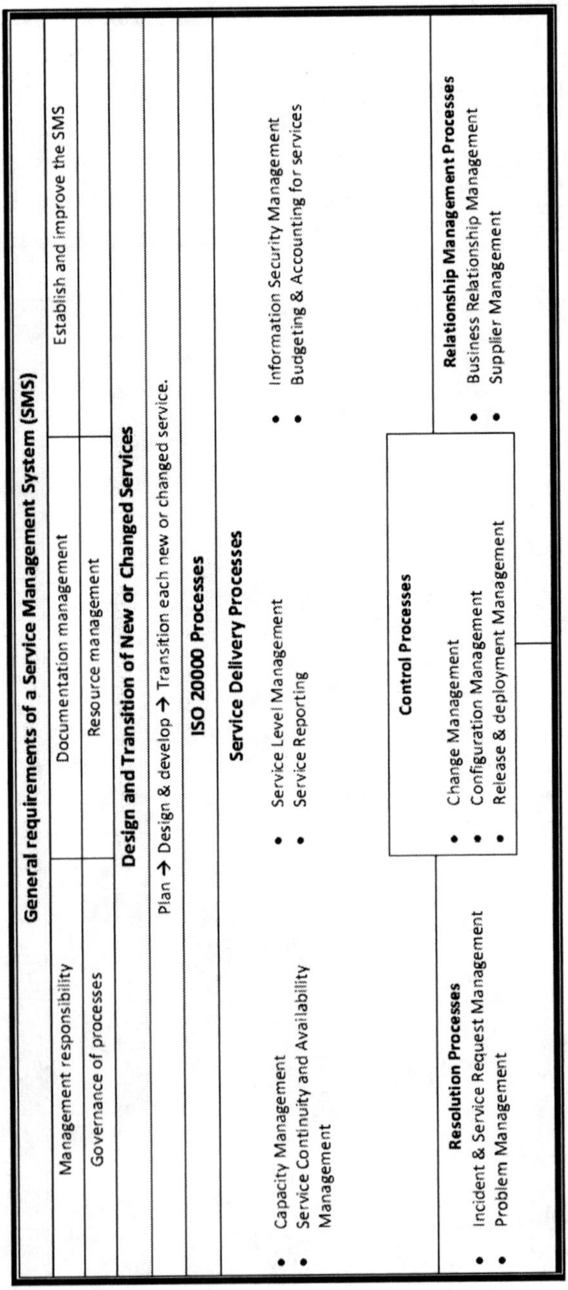

Figure 2.1: Service management system (SMS) for ISO/IEC 20000: 2011

The 13 processes used in ISO/IEC 20000: 2011 are referenced by COBIT 5 as being guidance for 13 of the COBIT 5 processes. *See Appendix A.*

Project Management

In this section the following will be discussed:

- PRINCE2® 2009 Edition
- PMBOK® 5th Edition (2013)

PRINCE2 2009 Edition

PRINCE2, an acronym for **PR**ojects **IN** Controlled Environments, was first published in 1996 and is a process-based method for managing projects of any kind. In 2009, it was upgraded to PRINCE2 2009 Edition to reflect developments in approaches to project management practices. In particular, it has reduced the number of processes and removed sub-processes, which are now called activities. It also discusses how PRINCE2 interacts with other frameworks from the UK Cabinet Office[19]: Managing Successful Programmes (MSP®) and Management of Risk (M_o_R®).

PRINCE2 is adopted worldwide as a project management framework and is the framework of choice for most organisations in Europe.

The processes in PRINCE2 2009 Edition are listed in *Table 2.3.*

---

[19] The UK Cabinet Office sold 51% of its ownership of Best Practice Frameworks to AXELOS in 2013. – really?

Table 2.3: PRINCE2 (2009) Processes

PRINCE2 Processes
Directing a Project
Starting up a Project
Initiating a Project
Managing Stage Boundaries
Controlling a Stage
Managing Product Delivery
Closing a Project
Planning

PRINCE2 is referenced by COBIT 5 as providing guidance for two of the 37 COBIT 5 processes – *see Appendix A*.

PMBOK®

PMBOK®, the **P**roject **M**anagement **B**ody of **K**nowledge, was first published in 1987 but in 2013 was updated to PMBOK® – 5th Edition.

PMBOK® – 5th Edition has five process areas:

1. Initiating (two processes)
2. Planning (24 processes)
3. Executing (eight processes)
4. Monitoring and Controlling (11 processes)
5. Closing (two processes)

and 10 Knowledge Areas.

1. Project Integration Management
2. Project Scope Management
3. Project Time Management

4. Project Cost Management
5. Project Quality Management
6. Project Human Resource Management
7. Project Communications Management
8. Project Risk Management
9. Project Procurement Management
10. Project Stakeholders Management *may want to check this out*

Each Knowledge Area contains processes that are part of the five Process Groups. In total PMBOK® – 5th Edition has 47 processes (five new processes were added). The Knowledge Area called Project Stakeholder Management is a new addition to the 5th Edition. It increases the focus on identification and engagement of stakeholders.

PMBOK® is adopted worldwide as a project management framework and it is the framework of choice in North America.

PMBOK® is referenced by COBIT 5 as providing guidance for three of the 37 COBIT 5 processes – *see Appendix A*.

Risk Management

From an IT governance perspective, risk management frameworks are designed to identify and analyse IT-related risks and determine how to mitigate, manage and monitor them while ensuring there is alignment with enterprise risk management.

There are many standards and frameworks covering risk management including:

- COSO ERM[20] (Enterprise Risk Management (2004) from the Committee of the Sponsoring Organisation of the Treadway Commission.
- Risk IT™[21] (2009) from ISACA. One of the ISACA frameworks used to build COBIT 5.
- Management of Risk (M_o_R)[22] (2002 with latest 2010) from The Cabinet Office[23].
- OCTAVE®[24] (2001 and onwards) (Operationally Critical Threat, Asset and Vulnerability Evaluation) from the Software Engineering Institute at Carnegie Mellon University.
- ISO 31000:2009 Risk Management – Principles and Guidelines. It covers principles, a risk management framework and a risk management process shown in *Figure 2.2*.

ISO31000 is referenced by COBIT 5 as being guidance for one of the COBIT 5 processes. *See Appendix A*.

---

[20] *www.coso.org/documents/COSO_ERM_ExecutiveSummary.pdf*
[21] *www.ISACA.org/Knowledge-Center/Research/ResearchDeliverables/Pages/The-Risk-IT-Framework.aspx*
[22] *www.mor-officialsite.com/*
[23] The UK Cabinet Office sold 51% of its ownership of Best Practice frameworks to AXELOS in 2013.
[24] *www.cert.org/octave/*

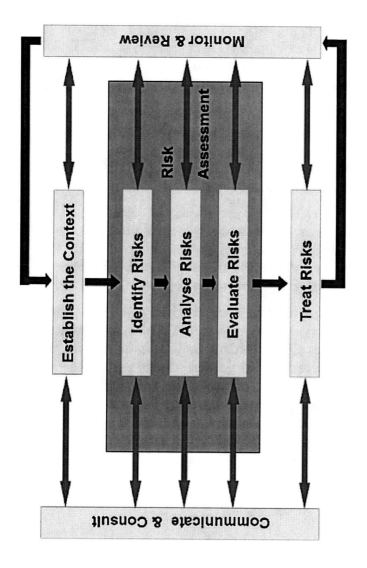

Figure 2.2: ISO31000 Risk Management Process (After ISO/IEC 31000)

Value Delivery

Value delivery enables business benefits to be realised from IT investments.

Value delivery frameworks are:

Val IT™ V2.0[25] (2008) from ISACA. One of the ISACA frameworks used to build COBIT 5.

Management of Value (MoV™)[26] (2010) from the UK Cabinet Office[27].

Information Security

Information security is principally covered by the ISO/IEC 27000 series of standards, although readers may find it interesting to look into two other frameworks that are related to ISO27000: MEHARI[28] and The Standard of Good Practice for Information Security.

MEHARI was developed originally in 1996 for chief information security officers, CIOs, risk managers and auditors by CLUSIF (Club de la securité de l'information français), based in Paris, France. It provides a comprehensive set of tools for risk analysis and risk management principally covering information security. It includes a risk assessment model and a security services reference manual for building a security framework. The latest version (2010) is aligned with ISO27002.

---

[25]   www.ISACA.org/Knowledge-Center/Research/ResearchDeliverables/Pages/Val-IT-Framework-2.0.aspx

[26] www.best-management-practice.com/Value-Management-MoV/

[27]UK Cabinet Office sold 51% of its Best Practice Frameworks such as MoV™ to AXELOS in 2013.

[28] www.clusif.asso.fr/en/clusif/present/

2: Key Frameworks and Standards Supporting Governance of Enterprise IT

The Standard of Good Practice for Information Security (2013)[29] from the Information Security Forum (ISF), founded in 1989, is a highly readable, annually updated and practical 372-page book that addresses information security from a business perspective.

The ISO27000 series[30] consists of a large number of standards of which two: ISO/IEC 27001 and ISO27002 are the main parts. Also, recently published in 2012, ISO/IEC 27013 explains how to integrate the implementation of ISO/IEC 27001 and ISO/IEC 20000:

ISO/IEC 27000: 2012. Information technology. Security techniques. Information security management systems. Overview and vocabulary.

ISO/IEC 27001: 2013. Information technology. Security techniques. Information security management systems. Requirements.

ISO/IEC 27002: 2013. Information technology. Security techniques. Code of practice for information security management.

ISO/IEC 27003: 2010. Information technology. Security techniques. Information security management system implementation guidance.

ISO/IEC 27004: 2009. Information technology. Security techniques. Information security management. Measurement.

ISO/IEC 27005: 2008. Information technology. Security techniques. Information security risk management.

---

[29] www.securityforum.org/shop/p-71-167
[30] www.iso27001security.com/html/iso27000.html

ISO/IEC 27006: 2011. Information technology. Security techniques. Requirements for bodies providing audit and certification of information security management systems.

ISO/IEC 27011: 2008. Information technology. Security techniques. Information security management guidelines for telecommunications organisations based on ISO/IEC 27002.

ISO/IEC 27013: 2012. Information technology. Security techniques. Guidance on the integrated implementation of ISO/IEC 27001 and ISO/IEC 20000-1.

ISO/IEC 27031: 2011. Information technology. Security techniques. Guidelines for information and communication technology readiness for business continuity.

ISO/IEC 27032: 2012. Information technology. Security techniques. Guidelines for cybersecurity.

ISO/IEC 27033-5: 2013. Information technology. Security techniques. Network security. Securing communications across networks using Virtual Private Networks (VPNs).

ISO/IEC 27034-1: 2011. Information technology. Security techniques. Application security. Overview and concepts.

ISO/IEC 27035: 2011. Information technology. Security techniques. Information security incident management.

ISO/IEC 27037: 2012. Information technology. Security techniques. Guidelines for identification, collection, acquisition and preservation of digital evidence.

ISO/IEC 27001 is referenced by COBIT®5 as being guidance for five of the COBIT®5 processes. *See Appendix A*.

Enterprise Architecture (EA)

Enterprise architecture is a framework, first established 25 years ago, that enables business strategy to be achieved using information systems and information technology by specifying how business processes across the enterprise will be developed and standardised to use information systems and information technology. Enterprise architecture can be viewed as a set of domains. There are several enterprise architecture frameworks and each has a slightly different view of the domains, but the general principles are similar.

Enterprise architecture domains can be summarised as shown in *Table 2.4*.

Table 2.4: Enterprise Architecture Layers (Based on TOGAF® 9.1)

Enterprise Architecture Domain	Description
Business architecture	Processes used by the business to meet its business strategy, governance and business outcomes
Application architecture	How specific applications are designed to conduct business processes and how they interact with one another
Data architecture	How the enterprise databases (or data warehouse) are organised and accessed by applications
Technical architecture	Hardware and software infrastructure including networks that supports applications and their interactions

Enterprise architectures commonly used are:

- TOGAF® – The Open Group Architecture Framework[31]
- Zachman Framework for Enterprise Architecture[32]
- CEAF – Commission Enterprise Architecture Framework[33]
- FEA – Federal Enterprise Architecture[34]

A comparison of three of these enterprise architectures was provided by Microsoft in 2007[35], although it did not include CEAF.

ISACA states in the *COBIT 5: Enabling Processes* book that TOGAF® 9 provides related guidance for two of the 37 COBIT 5 processes – *see Appendix A*. In addition, *COBIT 5: A Business Framework for the Governance and Management of Enterprise IT* also states that FEA and CEAF in addition to TOGAF® were used as inputs to COBIT 5.

Quality

Historically, there have been many frameworks and standards concerned with quality and all of them are still widely used:

- The Deming Cycle[36] – post Second World War from the US and into Japan, particularly. Known by everyone as Plan – Do – Check – Act (PDCA).

---

[31] *www.opengroup.org/togaf/*
[32] *www.intervista-institute.com/resources/zachman-poster.pdf*
[33] *http://ec.europa.eu/dgs/informatics/ecomm/doc/ceaf_guide_v1_1.pdf*
[34] *www.whitehouse.gov/sites/default/files/omb/assets/fea_docs/FEA_CRM_v23_Final_Oct_2007_Revised.pdf*
[35] *http://msdn.microsoft.com/en-us/library/bb466232.aspx*

2: Key Frameworks and Standards Supporting Governance of Enterprise IT

- Juran's Managerial Breakthrough[37] – mid-1960s, also in Japan.
- Kaizen[38] – the Kanji (Japanese) word for improvement also started post Second World War in Japan.
- Total Quality Management (TQM)[39] devised by Feigenbaum and based on PDCA.
- Six Sigma[40] – 1981 at Motorola in Japan.
- Baldridge National Quality Program (BNQP)[41] – 1987 as an excellence award for quality in the US.
- Lean[42] – late 1980s in Toyota, Japan. Often used with Six Sigma, now as Lean Six Sigma[43], devised in 2002.
- European Framework for Quality Management (EFQM)[44] – 1992 and notable for recognising continual improvement before it appeared in ISO9000.
- ISO9000[45] – originally 1987, based on BS5750 (1979), but currently ISO 9001: 2008 – notably devised the Quality Management System (QMS)

ISO9001 is referenced by COBIT 5 as being guidance for one of the COBIT 5 processes. *See Appendix A.*

---

[36] http://ocw.mit.edu/courses/engineering-systems-division/esd-60-lean-six-sigma-processes-summer-2004/lecture-notes/6_3_pdca.pdf
[37] http://books.google.co.uk/books/about/Juran_s_quality_handbook.html?id=beVTAAAAMAAJ&redir_esc=y
[38] http://uk.kaizen.com
[39] http://searchcio.techtarget.com/definition/Total-Quality-Management
[40] www.motorolasolutions.com/web/Business/_Moto_University/_Documents/_Static_Files/What_is_SixSigma.pdf
[41] www.nist.gov/baldrige
[42] www.lean.org/whatslean
[43] www.amazon.co.uk/What-Lean-Sigma-Michael-George/dp/007142668X
[44] www.efqm.org/the-efqm-excellence-model
[45] www.iso.org/iso/iso_9000

29

Maturity Assessment

In this section the following will be discussed:

- CMM®
- CMMI®
- ISO/IEC 15504

CMM®

The Software Engineering Institute (SEI) at Carnegie Mellon University, having initially devised a capability maturity model in 1986[46] to assess software development projects for the US Department of Defense, then published in 1993 the full Capability Maturity Model (CMM®), a maturity assessment framework for assessment of software development projects.

It was soon recognised by many people that the CMM® approach could be used for general business and IT process assessment and this was the approach used by ISACA to create the COBIT Maturity Model that was used for all COBIT processes up to and including COBIT 4.1.

CMMI®

In 2002, SEI superseded CMM® with Capability Maturity Model Integration (CMMI®)[47] to extend to other activities, not only software development.

The following are the current versions of CMMI® (2010):

---

[46] Humphrey, W. S. (1988), 'Characterizing the software process: A maturity framework' *IEEE Software* 5 (2), pp. 73–79.
[47] *http://cmmiinstitute.com/cmmi-getting-started/*

- *CMMI-DEV* is used to assess and improve engineering and development processes in an organisation that develops products.
- *CMMI-SVC* is used to assess and improve management and service delivery processes in an organisation that develops, manages and delivers services.
- *CMMI-ACQ* is used to assess and improve supplier management processes in an organisation that deals with multiple suppliers for its business.

CMMI® fulfills the requirements of ISO15504.

ISO15504 Process Capability Model

Like CMM®, ISO15504 was initially designed to address assessment of software development.

It started as a framework called SPICE[48] (Software Process Improvement and Capability Determination), which was developed initially by an international working group, starting in 1993, for assessing and improving software development. This became the international Standard ISO15504 in 2004.

In particular, ISO15504 covers the assessment process and defines a process assessment model (PAM) that requires a process reference model (PRM) to be devised and specifies how the PRM should be structured. The Standard can be used for process capability assessment and for process improvement.

There is clearly competition between the well-established and respected CMMI® and the later-to-market ISO15504.

---

[48] SPICE is still used as a name and SPICE conferences are held annually: 2013 in Bremen, Germany.

Although CMMI® incorporates many of the concepts of ISO15504, it is not an international standard. ISACA, therefore, made the decision that COBIT 5 should use ISO15504 and in *Chapter 8* we discuss how ISO15504 is used to assess and improve COBIT 5 processes.

Internal Controls

Internal controls are put in place by enterprises to transmit governance policies throughout the enterprise to ensure fiduciary control of financial and accounting information, with the aim of meeting operational and profitability targets while complying with regulations.

COSO

A framework for internal control was established in 1992 by the Committee of the Sponsoring Organisation of the Treadway Commission (COSO). The latest version is *Internal Control–Integrated Framework* (2013)[49]. The framework is separate from, but complementary to, the COSO ERM framework for enterprise risk management.

COSO was seen as an important framework to include in COBIT when the first version of COBIT was being developed between 1991 and 1996.

COSO is referenced by COBIT 5 as providing guidance for four of the 37 COBIT 5 processes – *see Appendix A*.

Sarbanes-Oxley Act

The Sarbanes-Oxley Act (2002), known colloquially as SOX, was introduced in the US to control enterprise board

---

[49] *www.coso.org/documents/990025P_Executive_Summary_final_may20_e.pdf.*

activity following Enron and Worldcom frauds. It applies to enterprises registered on the New York Stock Exchange (NYSE) and NASDAQ Stock Market. Section 404[50] of SOX is important because it covers the assessment of internal controls on financial reporting. IT services are fundamental to the creation of financial reports and hence must have appropriate internal controls and be assessed. After SOX was published, ISACA produced a guide, *IT Control Objectives for Sarbanes-Oxley*, and COBIT has been recognised as the framework to use to meet SOX requirements and pass Public Company Accounting Oversight Board (PCAOB)[51] assessment.

Sarbanes-Oxley was identified by ISACA as being used to assist with the development of COBIT 5. ISACA plans to publish *Sarbanes-Oxley using COBIT 5* in the second quarter of 2014. This will be an updated version of the COBIT 4.1 version published in 2006.

Basel III Framework

Basel III[52], the 2010-11 update to Basel II, is a framework for internal control systems in banking organisations. It has to be implemented between 2013 and 2018 and has banks worldwide complying with it.

ISACA published a guide, *IT Control Objectives for Basel II* that used COBIT 4.1.

Basel III was identified by ISACA as being used to assist with the development of COBIT 5.

---

[50] *https://na.theiia.org/standards-guidance/Public%20Documents/Sarbanes-Oxley_Section_404_--_A_Guide_for_Management_2nd_edition_1_08.pdf.*
[51] *http://pcaobus.org/about/pages/default.aspx.*
[52] *http://www.bis.org/bcbs/basel3.htm.*

Cultural Change Enablement

Cultural change enablement is a process to ensure stakeholders recognise and are committed to the need to change their culture, ethics and behaviour in order to be able to change the way the enterprise operates. Cultural change enablement is vital in order to successfully implement any changes to an enterprise's business activities including changes to IT such as the desire to implement governance of enterprise IT (GEIT).

The most commonly adopted approach to cultural change enablement is Kotter's 8 Steps to Transformation[53].

Kotters 8 steps are:

1. Establish a sense of urgency of the need for change
2. Form a guiding coalition of stakeholders
3. Create a vision of where the enterprise wants to be
4. Communicate the vision to everyone
5. Empower people to act
6. Plan and implement quick wins
7. Consolidate improvements and make further changes
8. Institutionalise the changes

Kotter's 8 steps have been used by ITIL for more than a decade and ISACA introduced it during COBIT 4.1 for implementing the governance of enterprise IT.

Kotter's cultural change enablement was identified by ISACA as being used to assist with the development of COBIT 5.

---

[53] Kotter, J.P., (1996), *Leading Change*, Boston, Harvard Business School Press.

2: Key Frameworks and Standards Supporting Governance of Enterprise IT

Semiotic Framework

COBIT 5 has an Information Model which includes the Semiotic Framework.

Semiotic Framework (or Semiotic Ladder)

Here are the steps, or layers (*Table 2.5*), based on Stamper's[54] Semiotic Ladder that is discussed in detail in *Chapter 5*.

Table 2.5: Steps (i.e. Layers) of the Semiotic Ladder

Social World	social aspects
Pragmatic	usage
Semantic	meaning
Syntactic	structure
Empiric	information access channel
Physical World	information carrier/media

Stamper, in 1973, recognised that he needed to update Morris' (1938)[55] semiotic model of Syntactic, Semantic and Pragmatic layers to take into account the introduction of information technology. Stamper added Empiric and Physical levels so that information theory introduced by

---

[54] Stamper, R. K. (1973), *Information in Business and Administrative Systems*, London, Batsford.
[55] Morris, C. (1938), 'Foundations of the Theory of Signs'. *International Encyclopedia of Unified Science*, ed. Neurath, O., Chicago, University of Chicago Press, Vol. 1, No. 2. (Reprint: Chicago, University of Chicago Press, 1970-71), Reprint: Morris, C., *Writings on the General Theory of Signs*, The Hague, Mouton, 1971, pp. 13–71).

Shannon[56] in 1948 was incorporated, that is, the physics of signs, that is, the hardware used to transmit, receive and process them and the empirics of signs that covers patterns, variety, noise, channel capacity, codes and so on. The ladder from Physical World to Social World covers data (Empiric and Syntactic) and information (Semantic and Pragmatic) that becomes knowledge in the Social World. The Physical World is where everything that can be empirically observed takes place. Information structures at the Pragmatic level is used to construct Social World activities such as creation and agreement of contracts, interpretation of a business case or management decision making based on balanced scorecard reports.

Business Continuity Management

The International Standard ISO22301:2012 (formerly a British Standard BS25999-2 published in 2007) specifies the requirements for a Business Continuity Management System (BCMS) to protect a business from disruptive incidents in addition to reducing the likelihood that such incidents might occur. Like other management system standards, ISO22301 uses Plan, Do, Check, Act (PDCA) as its core approach with key activities that cover business impact analysis (BIA), strategy, planning, exercising and improvement.

BS25999-2:2007 is referenced by COBIT 5 as being guidance for one of the COBIT 5 processes. *See Appendix A.*

---

[56] Shannon, C.E. (1948), 'A Mathematical Theory of Communication', *The Bell Systems Technical Journal*, 27, pp. 379–423, 623–656. Available at *http://cm.bell-labs.com/cm/ms/what/shannonday/shannon1948.pdf* (Accessed 5 September 2013).

CHAPTER 3: COBIT – FROM IT AUDIT TO GEIT

'History is the version of past events that people have decided to agree upon.'

Napoleon Bonaparte
(1769-1821)

This brief chapter looks at the history of COBIT.

Accurate reporting on the early history of COBIT comes from Erik Guldentops, now Executive Professor at the University of Antwerp Management School (UAMS), who is recognised as the 'grandfather of COBIT'. Guldentops told us[57] that it was in Paris in 1991 at a meeting of ISACA's European Regional Council that he was invited to conduct research to devise a European IT audit initiative since IT audit knowledge at that time came only from the US. At that time, Guldentops was Chief Inspector at SWIFT, the international funds transfer body, where he went on to be Director Information Security. His article also lists the names of the group of 34 people led by himself who developed the first version of COBIT that was issued in 1996. He also points out that it was the Electronic Data Processing Auditors Association (EDPAA's) Control Objectives that drove his research (probably, in my view, explaining why COBIT was originally called **C**ontrol **OB**jectives for **I**nformation and related **T**echnology). Today, COBIT is just a word, no longer an acronym, since

---

[57] www.isaca.org/Journal/Past-Issues/2011/Volume-4/Documents/jpdf11v4-Where-Have-All.pdf

COBIT 5 is a business framework for the governance and management of enterprise IT.

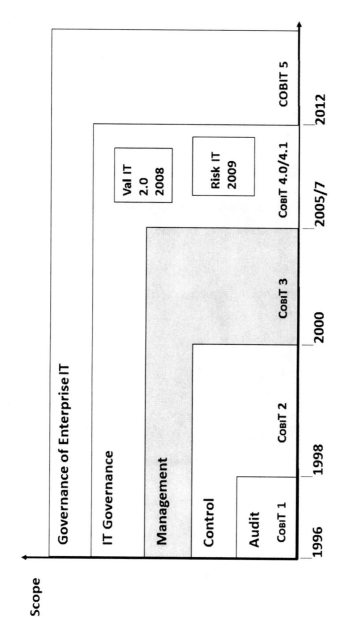

Figure 3.1: COBIT®: Audit to GEIT in 16 years

Figure 3.1 shows COBIT was initially developed as an IT audit framework and in today's view of history[58] is seen as moving over 16 years from IT audit (COBIT 1) to IT control (COBIT 2) to IT management (COBIT 3) to IT governance (COBIT 4.0/4.1) to governance of enterprise IT (GEIT) (COBIT 5). *Table 3.1* is a comparison of the versions of COBIT since 1996. Additional benefits could be obtained if COBIT 4.0 or COBIT 4.1 were enhanced by the implementation of other ISACA frameworks: Val IT™ 2.0, which had processes to aid delivery of value from IT, and Risk IT™, which had processes to aid risk management.

---

[58] *www.isaca.org/Knowledge-Center/cobit/Pages/Development.aspx*

Table 3.1: Comparisons of Versions of COBIT® Since 1996

Version Name	Date	Domain Names	Number of Processes	Number of Control Objectives (Practices)	Comments
COBIT	April 1996	Planning and Organisation Acquisition and Implementation Delivery and Support Monitoring	(32)	271	Designed for IS audit purposes
COBIT 2nd Edition	April 1998	Planning and Organisation Acquisition and Implementation Delivery and Support Monitoring	11 6 13 4 (34)	302 detailed 34 high-level	
COBIT 3rd Edition	July 2000	Planning and Organisation (PO) Acquisition and Implementation (AI) Delivery and Support (DS) Monitoring (M)	11 6 13 4 (34)	318 detailed 34 high-level	Management guidelines and Maturity Methods added
COBIT 4	4.0 Dec 2005 4.1 May 2007	Plan and Organise (PO) Acquire and Implement (AI) Deliver and Support (DS) Monitor and Evaluate	10 7 13 4 (34)	4.0: 215 4.1: 210	Verbs replace nouns in process names:
COBIT 5	April 2012	Evaluate, Direct and Monitor (EDM) Align, Plan and Organise (APO) Build, Acquire and Implement (BAI) Deliver, Service and support (DSS) Monitor, Evaluate and Access (MEA)	5 13 10 6 3 (37)	Governance practices (15) Management Practices (195)	Separation of governance & management. 210 practices in total

CHAPTER 4: OVERVIEW OF COBIT 5 – GOVERNANCE OF ENTERPRISE IT

'If I have seen further it is by standing on the shoulders of giants.'

Isaac Newton
(1643-1727)

This chapter explains the basic concepts that make up COBIT 5.

Why COBIT 5 was developed

Within a year of COBIT 4.1 being published in May 2007, the international Standard ISO/IEC 38500: 2008 Corporate Governance of IT was published. It was at this point that some ISO/IEC 38500 insiders started to express in public that the COBIT 4.1 framework which incorporated powerful IT governance approaches such as business goals driving IT goals driving IT processes was really only IT management rather than IT governance. This concern was addressed in February 2009 by an article by Gary Hardy, one of the founders of COBIT. His article, *ITGI Enables ISO/IEC 38500:2008 Adoption*[59], demonstrated how ITGI's family of products, in particular COBIT and Val IT™, provided the support for IT governance according to ISO/IEC 38500. Hardy's article showed how ISACA's frameworks of COBIT 4.1, Val IT™ and related guidance support the six principles (responsibility, strategy, acquisition, performance, conformance and human

---

[59] Hardy, G (2009), *ITGI Enables ISO/IEC 38500:2008 Adoption*, Rolling Meadows, Illinois, ISACA®

behaviour) and the three main tasks (evaluate, direct and monitor) of the ISO/IEC 38500 Standard. The debate died down, but clearly once an international Standard for the corporate governance of IT was in place, COBIT would need to take it on board at its next major upgrade. Now COBIT 5 has been published, ISACA admits that COBIT 4.1's domains have evolved into the management domains of COBIT 5[60] and that a new governance domain has been created too.

Fascinating as that challenge to COBIT 4.1 may have been, it was not the only reason for upgrading the COBIT framework. A major factor that all committees responsible for international standards and frameworks recognise is that about every five years, they need to review their international standard or framework to take into account developments in the world and by 'standing on the shoulders of giants'[61] – that is, advance by using new or changed concepts developed by others.

What COBIT 5 addresses

ISACA decided its next generation of guidance covered by COBIT 5 should cover the governance and management of enterprise IT (GEIT) and should address the following:

- Integrate into COBIT 5 all ISACA's frameworks and guidance, principally COBIT®4.1, Val IT V2.0 and Risk IT™ but also the Business Model for Information Security (BMIS™), the IT Assurance Framework

---

[60] ISACA® (2012), *COBIT® 5: Enabling Processes*, Rolling Meadows, Illinois, ISACA®, p. 24.
[61] A historical saying but most famously used by physicist Sir Isaac Newton in his letter to physicist Robert Hooke, in 1676.

(ITAF™), the Board Briefing on IT Governance (2nd Edition) publication and the Taking Governance Forward (TGF) research.

- Take on board other major frameworks and standards such as those discussed in *Chapter 2*.
- Take into account the pervasive nature of IT in businesses today and the increasing growth and dependency of businesses on other businesses, on IT organisations including outsourcing, reliance on suppliers, other service providers and consultants.
- Put in place an information model to deal with the significant increase in information[62] and the need, not only to manage information but also to select appropriate information to make effective business decisions.
- Recognise that increased guidance is required to cover innovation that is increasingly based on emerging technologies and is vital for businesses to remain efficient and effective as well as extend their customer base.
- Cover not just IT processes but also ensure end-to-end business and IT functional responsibilities are addressed by the provision of governance and management of enterprise IT using organisational structures, policies and culture.
- Ensure the delivery of enterprise IT is fully engaged with the business to ensure core business expectations are achieved:
  - Value creation
  - Business user satisfaction

---

[62] Fashionably known as 'Big Data'.

- Regulatory and contractual compliance
- Recognise that controls are needed to effectively handle the growth in user-initiated and user-controlled IT solutions – such as Bring Your Own Device (BYOD).

Key Ideas of COBIT 5

COBIT 5 is based simply on two concepts:

- Five principles
- Seven enablers (*see Chapter 5*)

The Five Principles

The five principles explain exactly what COBIT 5 has been designed to achieve:

1. Meeting stakeholder needs
2. Covering the enterprise end-to-end
3. Applying a single integrated framework
4. Enabling a holistic approach
5. Separating governance from management

Principle 1: Meeting stakeholder needs

Stakeholders are both internal and external. Internal stakeholders are roles given to members of the enterprise and range across the levels of the enterprise and include the board; CEO; CFO; business executives and managers; risk, security and audit managers; IT managers; and users. External stakeholders are not members of the enterprise and roles include, but are not limited to, shareholders, business partners, suppliers, regulatory officials, external auditors and customers.

Enterprises are expected to create value for their stakeholders and that is the reason why the key governance objective of an enterprise is value creation. Value creation is perceived as realising benefits at optimal resource costs while optimising[63] risks (*Figure 4.1*).

The cogs of optimising resources and optimising risks together assist benefits realisation. It is the stakeholder needs that determine what the value should be and different stakeholders have different needs. Therefore, the governance system should take into account all stakeholder needs when making decisions.

Figure 4.1 Value Creation

---

[63] The term *optimising risks* is not liked by everyone since in many dictionaries risks are defined as negatives such as hazards or losses and so people feel *minimising risks* is a more conventional term. However, ISO/IEC 31000 (Risk management) defines risk as 'effect of uncertainty on objectives' and therefore covers both positives such as increased revenue or improved management, as well as negatives such as security breaches or loss of key staff. Therefore *optimising risks* is the term to use.

Stakeholder needs are driven by many factors both internal and external. External factors are what is changing in the world: politics, economies, social factors, technology, laws and the environment[64] together with what shareholders, citizens or customers want and what competitors are doing. Internal factors include the nature of the organisation in terms of its culture, its strategy, its mission and vision statements, and its risk appetite. Governance, therefore, needs to understand stakeholder needs in order to successfully determine decisions on benefits, risks and resources in order to customise governance. COBIT 5 has evaluated how stakeholder needs map to enterprise goals, IT-related goals and enabler goals. This is the COBIT 5 Goals Cascade that is covered later in this chapter.

Principle 2: Covering the enterprise end-to-end

In the past decade, it has been universally recognised that IT is a fundamental part of running an enterprise and realising benefits. It has always been recognised that the board and executive management are responsible for finance and human resource governance and now enterprise governance of IT too – as ISO/IEC 38500 (Corporate Governance of IT) made absolutely clear.

Figure 4.2a shows how the Board conducts governance of finance. The Board is responsible for governance of finance and therefore evaluates internal and external drivers and current performance and makes decisions on strategy, return on investment (ROI), solvency and value. The Board directs by allocation of responsibility and targets to management teams in the enterprise. The chief finance

---

[64] Commonly called PESTLE, the first letters of the words.

officer (CFO) is the person responsible for controlling finance and provides policy and objectives on finance to management teams in the enterprise. Management teams in the enterprise are responsible for providing performance in financial terms and they have an enabler in that the finance department of the enterprise assists them with understanding and managing costs, budgets, profits and ROI.

Reporting from management to the CFO is in detail but the CFO's reporting to the Board is of a summary nature. The Board monitors financial results in the CFO's reports and evaluates and directs management based on the monitoring.

Figure 4.2b takes a similar approach to demonstrate how the Board conducts governance of IT. As with governance of finance, the Board determines strategy, ROI, value and solvency and the Board directs by allocation of responsibility and targets to management teams in the enterprise. The chief information officer (CIO) is responsible for controlling IT and provides policies and objectives on IT to management teams in the enterprises. Management teams in the enterprise are responsible for the delivery of performance by their business unit and IT is essential for delivery. They request new IT services to be provided and they use existing IT services, and the enabler is the IT department. Reports from management teams in the enterprise to the CIO are reports on IT services and its impact on business performance (operational records), which comes directly from IT departments as well as from management teams. The CIO then provides operational reports to the Board that indicate operational business performance and the outcome benefits of investments (i.e. from IT projects). The Board monitors these reports and evaluates and directs the management teams as necessary.

[handwritten margin note: what do CIO is resp fr]

[handwritten margin note: is general]

[handwritten note at bottom: OK - here is a tough pt w/ operations mgmt → and desire to eliminate unnecessary waste.]

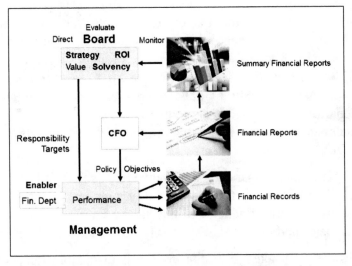

Figure 4.2a: Board Governance of Finance

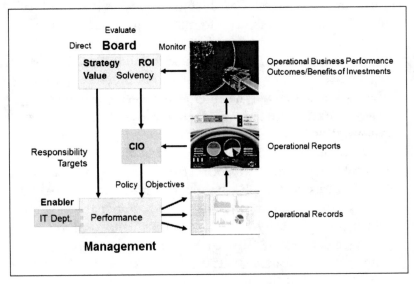

Figure 4.2b: Board Governance of IT

COBIT 5 addresses governance and management of IT from such an end-to-end perspective. Enterprise governance of IT is integrated into enterprise governance as just discussed. In addition, COBIT 5 addresses all the relevant internal and external IT services in addition to internal and external business processes. COBIT 5 states that 'it provides a holistic and systemic view on governance and management of enterprise IT based on a number of enablers.' As will become clear later in this chapter, when the seven categories of COBIT 5 enablers are discussed, these seven COBIT 5 enablers cover in detail the requirements that ensure the enabler in *Figure 4.2b*, the IT department, is using good practices and meets its goals.

The end-to-end governance approach of COBIT 5 in *Figure 4.3* has these key components:

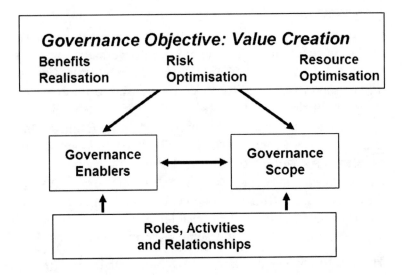

Figure 4.3: Governance and Management Approach of COBIT 5

(This figure is derived from Figure 8, p.23 of *COBIT 5: A business framework for the governance and management of enterprise IT*).

- Governance Objective: Value Creation consisting of benefits realisation, risk optimisation and resource optimisation (*see Principle 1*).
- Governance Enablers, which are the seven Enablers (*see Principle 4*) that enable an enterprise to create value.
- Governance Scope, which means the part of the enterprise to which governance is applied. This can be the entire enterprise or part of it, referred to by COBIT 5 as 'an entity, a tangible or intangible asset etc.' In some enterprises, governance may be applied differently in different parts, for example, a major enterprise that is a group of companies which operate in very different business sectors.

- Roles, Activities and Relationships (*Figure 4.4*[65]) shows the four major roles and their interactions:
  - Owners and stakeholders
  - The governing body
  - Management
  - Operations and execution

This is conformant with the view of corporate governance of Barger (2004) that was discussed in *Chapter 1*.

---

[65] This diagram is very similar to Barger's diagram (*Figure 1.1 in Chapter 1*) but has been rotated anticlockwise by 90° by ISACA[K], plus work by Operations and Execution has been added that supports the Management.

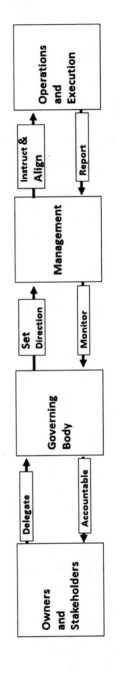

Figure 4.4: Roles, Activities and Relationships in an Enterprise
(This figure is derived from Figure 9, p.24 of *COBIT 5: A business framework for the governance and management of enterprise IT*).

Principle 3: Applying a single integrated framework

COBIT 5 has integrated the existing ISACA frameworks discussed earlier in this chapter and the wide range of other standards and frameworks that are relevant to the governance of enterprise IT that were discussed in *Chapter 2*. In that sense ISACA sees COBIT 5 as a single integrated framework that is a 'consistent and integrated source of guidance in a non-technical, technology-agnostic common language'.

Principle 4: Enabling a holistic approach

The holistic approach to delivering governance and management of enterprise IT is to implement enablers (*Figure 4.5*). COBIT 5 recognises the need for seven categories of enablers:

1. Principles, policies and frameworks
2. Processes
3. Organisational structures
4. Culture, ethics and behaviour
5. Information
6. Services, infrastructure and applications
7. People, skills and competencies

Collectively, the final three enablers (5, 6 and 7) are enterprise resources.

Principles 1+2 seem to be missing from this book - oops - go back to p.46 + p.48

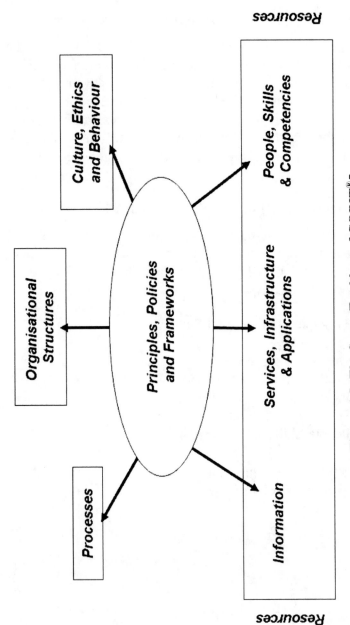

Figure 4.5: The Seven Enablers of COBIT®5
(This figure is derived from Figure 12. p.27 of *COBIT 5: A business framework for the governance and management of enterprise IT*).

It has long been recognised that processes alone will not successfully deliver governance and management of enterprise IT and other requirements are also needed. Other frameworks have recognised this too. For example, the ITIL framework (*see Chapter 2*), which is commonly seen to be a framework of IT service management processes, recognises that the implementation of ITIL processes will not be successful without having people with appropriate skills and competencies[66] and designing suitable organisational structures, called functions: IT operations management, technical management and applications management. ITIL also recognises that for ITIL implementation to be successful cultural change is essential to ensure IT staff recognise that IT service management is a customer service provider.

COBIT 5 has a comprehensive set of enablers that need to be interconnected. Each enabler may be an input to assist other enablers. Outputs of an enabler may assist other enablers. For example, in *Figure 4.6*, the COBIT 5 processes include the Manage Service Requests and Incidents (DSS02) process. Information needed for that process would be the user, their incident and the components affected. The process would be run by a Service Desk doing 1st-line management of the incident, with more technically skilled IT staff running 2nd-line and 3rd-line support (i.e. the organisational structure). The people in 1st, 2nd and 3rd-line roles need appropriate skills and competencies to conduct the DSS02 process. The information output from the process would include the steps that resolved the incident and the time taken to

---

[66] Rudd, C. (2010), ITIL V3: *Planning to Implement Service Management*, London, The Stationery Office.

resolve the incident. That information would act as information for the services, infrastructure and applications enabler to assist with recognition that service levels can be met. Detailed discussion of the seven COBIT 5 enablers is the content of *Chapter 5*.

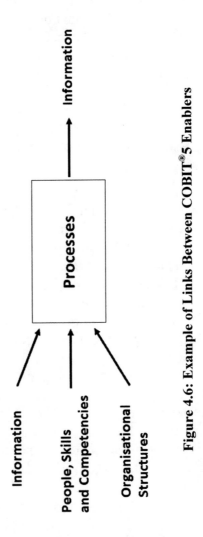

Figure 4.6: Example of Links Between COBIT®5 Enablers

Principle 5: Separating governance from management

The COBIT 5 framework adheres to the principle of corporate governance that governance and management are separate (see *Chapter 1*), or put more specifically they are distinct but communicate.

COBIT 5 defines governance as:

'**Governance** ensures that stakeholder needs, conditions and options are evaluated to determine:

- balanced, agreed-on enterprise objectives to be achieved;
- setting direction through prioritisation and decision making;
- and monitoring performance and compliance against agreed-on direction and objectives.'

Management is defined as:

'**Management** plans, builds, runs and monitors activities in alignment with the direction set by the governance body to achieve the enterprise objectives.'

COBIT 5's view is that governance is the responsibility of the board of directors with leadership from the chairperson. In reality, the board of directors is accountable (rather than responsible) for governance. Note that although the board of directors retains accountability for governance it is perfectly acceptable for them to appoint an IT Strategy

Committee (sometimes called IT Steering Committee)[67] to be responsible for governance.

In a few countries in the world the board of directors has a different name. For example, in the Netherlands, the Management Board consists of managing directors. Its members can be compared to the executive members of a board of directors in the UK or the US. However, it is possible, but not compulsory, for most enterprises to also have a Supervisory Board that oversees the Management Board (Loyens & Loeff, 2007)[68].

COBIT 5's view is that management is the responsibility of executive management under the leadership of the CEO. Executive management (*aka* senior management) is immediately beneath the board of directors and is responsible for the day-to-day activities of the enterprise and is usually led by the CEO who is often also an internal member of the board of directors.

As we have seen, governance is about evaluation, direction and monitoring and this requires interaction with management that plans, builds, runs and monitors the enterprise activities (*Figure 4.7*). The processes that cover governance and management outlined in *Figure 4.7* are described in the COBIT 5 Process Reference Model (PRM) – *see Appendix B*. The PRM provides 37 processes and separates these into governance and management areas.

---

[67] According to van Grembergen (2009), an IT Strategy Committee is at Board of Directors' level whereas an IT Steering Committee is at executive management level. However, few organisations have both committees.

[68] *www.loyensloeff.com/en-US/AboutUs/CountryDesks/Documents/legal_aspects_of_doing_business_in_the_netherlands.pdf.*

Overall there are five domains:

Governance: the single domain Evaluate, Direct and Monitor (EDM) consisting of five processes.

Management: four domains

- Align, Plan and Organise (APO) consisting of 13 processes
- Build, Acquire and Implement (BAI) consisting of 10 processes
- Deliver, Service and Support consisting of 6 processes
- Monitor, Evaluate and Assess (MEA) consisting of 3 processes

The PRM consists of what COBIT 5 sees as all the processes relating to IT activities that are normally found in an enterprise. The 37 processes are comprehensive, but there may still be other processes that an enterprise considers they require to meet its stakeholder needs.

Enterprises will select COBIT 5 processes to use that are appropriate and it is quite likely that small enterprises will use fewer processes than large enterprises. What is important to recognise is that all enterprises will select their own set of processes that best assists them to deliver the governance of enterprise IT.

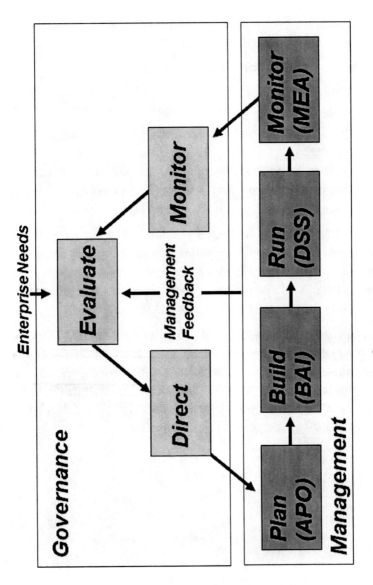

Figure 4.7: COBIT®5 Governance and Management Areas
(This figure is derived from Figure 15, p.32 of COBIT 5: A business framework for the governance and management of enterprise IT).

COBIT 5 Goals Cascade

ISACA has used almost a decade of research, conducted by its IT Governance Institute (ITGI) arm studying enterprises of all sizes worldwide, to develop the concept of a goals cascade that allows assessment based on knowledge of enterprise goals being mapped to IT-related goals and then mapping IT-related goals to COBIT processes. This goals cascade assists enterprises to recognise key COBIT processes.

For COBIT 5, the goals cascade has been extended and now it can (if required) be used to start with stakeholder needs and map those to the enterprise goals before mapping enterprise goals to IT-related goals and IT-related goals to COBIT processes. I have used this cascade approach for identifying key processes with several major clients in different countries for COBIT 4.1 and COBIT 5 and I would definitely recommend using this in your enterprise.

The COBIT 5 Goals Cascade is shown in *Figure 4.8*. It shows that Stakeholder Drivers arise from PESTLE changes[69] coupled with competitors' activities and this affects the Stakeholder Needs, which is what needs to be assessed. Assessment of Stakeholder Needs is best conducted by workshops with stakeholders to determine their needs.[70] It is not essential to start with Stakeholder Needs if you believe stakeholders have strong views on what the enterprise goals are; in that case the Goals Cascade can start with Enterprise Goals. The Enterprise

---

[69] Political, economic, social, technological, legal and environmental.
[70] Workshops can often be more effectively conducted if you and your business and IT colleagues build a 'straw man', which is your view on Stakeholder Needs and then use that as the basis for getting workshops of stakeholders to work from that 'straw man' towards what they believe are their stakeholder needs.

Goals are shown in *Table 4.9* and the IT-related Goals in *Table 4.10*. These are generics that have been devised from about a decade of research by ITGI.

Table 4.9: Enterprise Goals (Generic)

Perspective	No.	Enterprise Goal
Financial	1	Stakeholder value of business investments
	2	Portfolio of competitive products and services
	3	Managed business risk (safeguarding of assets)
	4	Compliance with external laws and regulations
	5	Financial transparency
Customer	6	Customer-oriented service culture
	7	Business service continuity and availability
	8	Agile responses to changing business environment
	9	Information-based strategic decision making
	10	Optimisation of service delivery costs
Internal	11	Optimisation of business process functionality
	12	Optimisation of business process costs
	13	Managed business change programmes
	14	Operational and staff productivity
	15	Compliance with internal policies
Learning and Growth	16	Skilled and motivated people
	17	Product and business innovation culture

Table 4.10: IT-related Goals (Generic)

Perspective	No.	IT-related Goal
Financial	1	Alignment of IT and business strategy
	2	IT compliance and support for business compliance with external laws and regulations
	3	Commitment of executive management for making IT-related decisions
	4	Managed IT-related business risk
	5	Realised benefits from IT-enabled investments and service portfolio
	6	Transparency of IT costs, benefits and risk
Customer	7	Delivery of IT services in line with business requirements
	8	Adequate use of applications, information and technology solutions
Internal	9	IT agility
	10	Security of information, processing infrastructure and applications
	11	Optimisation of IT assets, resources and capabilities
	12	Enablement and support of business processes by integrating applications and technology into business processes
	13	Delivery of programmes delivering benefits on time, on budget and meeting requirements and quality standards
	14	Availability of reliable and useful information for decision making
	15	IT compliance with internal policies
Learning and Growth	16	Competent and motivated business and IT personnel
	17	Knowledge, expertise and initiatives for business innovation

COBIT 5 has provided mapping tables that are shown in *Appendix C*:

- Stakeholder Needs mapped to Enterprise Goals: *Table C.1*
- Enterprise Goals mapped to IT-related Goals: *Table C.2*
- IT-related Goals mapped to COBIT 5 Enablers (which in Q3 2013 are still solely processes)[71]: Table *C.3*

It is also vital to recognise that finding the desired COBIT 5 processes to use is not all that is needed; other Enablers (discussed earlier in this chapter and in detail in *Chapter 5*) also need to be in place.

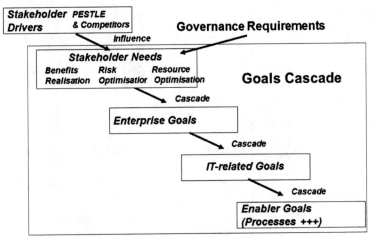

Figure 4.8: COBIT®5 Goals Cascade

---

[71] In Q4 2013 *COBIT®5: Enabling Information* from ISACA® is planned for publication and that is also expected to have a goals cascade with the Enabler Goal being Information.

What needs to be recognised is that a spreadsheet needs to be set up to use the mapping tables so that they can be used effectively. It is best to give weightings to Stakeholder Needs if those are the start of the Goals Cascade, or to give weightings to Enterprise Goals if you plan to start with Enterprise Goals. Also, your spreadsheet should allow different values to be added for the Primary (P) and Secondary (S) mappings shown in *Table C.2* and *Table C.3* so that your views on the relative importance of P and S can be considered. If you believe some of the mappings do not fit your enterprise then you are advised by experts in the team that devised the Goals Cascade to adjust the mappings accordingly. Finally, the Goals Cascade is not definitive like a mechanical device or a program – it is enterprise-related and the COBIT processes that arise from the Goals Cascade that are considered as important should still be compared and aligned with other approaches such as selecting COBIT processes that assist with meeting the enterprise's risk requirements or building on processes already in place. This is discussed further in *Chapter 8*.

CHAPTER 5: THE SEVEN ENABLERS OF COBIT 5

'All our dreams can come true – if we have the courage to pursue them.'

Walt Disney (1901-1966)

The seven COBIT 5 enablers were outlined in *Chapter 4* under *Principle 4: Enabling a holistic approach* where it was made clear that enablers need to work together if governance is to be achieved. This chapter discusses each of the seven categories of enablers in depth.

First of all, each enabler is expressed in terms of two concepts:

- Enabler Dimension
- Enabler Performance Management

Enabler Dimension

The word 'dimension' is used considerably by COBIT 5:

- Process Dimension
- Capability Dimension
- Enabler Dimension

Dimension is best understood as meaning 'aspects' or 'set of elements'.

Process Dimension covers the aspects of every COBIT 5 process in terms of their names, their purpose and their practices and so on.

The Capability Dimension covers the aspects of the Process Assessment Model (PAM) needed for assessing the capability of every process in terms of capability levels (0 to 5) and process attributes (PA) used to assess each level. This will be covered in *Chapter 9*.

Enabler Dimension covers aspects of every enabler and these aspects are:

- stakeholders,
- goals,
- lifecycle,
- good practices.

Stakeholders

Stakeholders are any people, internal to the enterprise or external, who are involved with, or have an interest in, the enabler. Examples of stakeholders are shown in *Table 5.1*.

Table 5.1: Examples of Enabler Stakeholders

Internal Stakeholders	External Stakeholders
Board of Directors	Shareholders
CEO, CFO, CIO, CRO, CISO, COO, CTO	Customers
Business executives, managers and business process owners	Business partners and suppliers
Risk and compliance managers	Regulators and standardisation bodies
Security managers	Consultants
Service managers	External auditors
Internal auditors	
IT managers	
IT users	

It is the stakeholders' needs that drive the enterprise goals that themselves determine the IT-related goals needed by the enterprise.

Goals

Enablers provide value to the enterprise by the achievement of goals. Each enabler goal is described in terms of three categories, as shown in *Table 5.2.*

Table 5.2: Enabler-goal Categories

Enabler category	Meaning
Intrinsic quality	Enabler works accurately and objectively providing reputable, accurate and objective results.
Contextual quality	Enabler is fit for purpose (i.e. displays relevance and effectiveness) in the context in which it is used. This means it will be understandable, easy to use and it will work and achieve outcomes completely, appropriately and consistently.
Access and Security	Enabler and its outcomes are accessible as required but also secured so that enabler outcomes are only accessible to those people who need and have been granted access.

Lifecycle

Each of the enablers has a lifecycle that starts with planning the introduction of the enabler, followed by operationally using it and then eventually disposing of it at the end of its lifetime. COBIT 5 provides a standard list of lifecycle phases, as shown in *Table 5.3*.

Table 5.3: Enabler Lifecycle Phases

Lifecycle phases
Plan
Design
Build/Acquire/Create/Implement
Use/Operate
Evaluate/Monitor
Update/Dispose

Good Practices

Each of the enablers needs to be defined in terms of the good practices it will use. COBIT 5 provides the good practices that should be used for some enablers such as Processes and Information – in the *COBIT 5: Enabling Processes* and the *COBIT 5: Enabling Information* manuals. For other enablers, guidance is provided from other standards, frameworks and academic research. For example, the good practices for the Culture, Ethics and Behaviour enabler is largely based on Kotter's (1996) textbook *Leading Change*.

Enabler Performance Management

Performance of enablers is managed in COBIT 5 through the assessment of each of the four enabler dimensions: stakeholders, goals, lifecycle and good practices.

Assessment is simply conducted by asking a question to determine whether each enabler dimension has been achieved and specifying metrics that can be used to measure the extent of the achievement, as shown in *Table 5.4.*

Table 5.4: Enabler Performance Management: Questions and Metrics

Enabler Dimension	Question	Metric	Metric Type
Stakeholders	Are stakeholders' needs addressed?	Metrics for achievement of goals	Lag indicator
Goals	Are enabler goals achieved?		Lag indicator
Lifecycle	Is lifecycle managed?	Metrics for application of practices	Lead indicator
Good Practices	Are good practices applied?		Lead indicator

Metrics that measure how successfully lifecycle management is taking place and how well good practices are being applied do not indicate that desired outcomes are being achieved, but they are likely to indicate that enablers are being successfully run, which is likely to lead to the desired stakeholder needs and enterprise goals being achieved. However, only measurement of the achievement of stakeholder needs and enterprise goals will actually indicate that is the case.

A good analogy for lead and lag indicators is the relationship between appraisals given by delegates at the end of a COBIT 5 training course and the exam results achieved by delegates. The trainer will look at the course appraisal sheets and if these are all very positive about the course then that will be a lead indicator to the trainer that the delegate pass rate on the COBIT 5 exam will be high. However, only on receipt of the COBIT 5 exam results (the lag indicator) will the delegate pass rate be known.

Enablers 1 - 7

Enabler 1: Principles, Policies and Frameworks

Principles are the governance body's expression of its fundamental values and assumptions that it uses to express its views concerning the beliefs of the enterprise and the directions it has intentions of driving to. Principles are used to communicate both internally and externally and to ensure sound stewardship of assets that belong to the shareholders of a commercial enterprise or citizens of a public sector enterprise. Principles can be viewed as an expansion of the mission and vision statements of an enterprise. Example documents that cover principles are: ethics charter and social responsibility charter. A social responsibility charter was devised by the World Bank as a document that stated: 'The commitment of business to contribute to sustainable economic development – working with employees, their families, the local community and society at large to improve the quality of life, in ways that are both good for business and good for development.' Principles should be brief and simple.

Based on principles, governance bodies provide policies to management to formally convey what has to be accomplished by management – that is, the policies are the rules and guidance on the overall intention and direction.

Frameworks are governance and management frameworks that ensure proper governance and management of enterprise IT by the provision of structure, guidance and tools. COBIT 5 is such a framework, of course. Policies need to be a part of the overall governance and management framework that itself is the structure into which all policies fit and links to the underlying principles of the enterprise.

Key points

Stakeholders:

Stakeholders define policies (internal stakeholders in governance roles) and comply with policies (internal and external stakeholders).

Goals:

Principles should be limited in number and written in simple language to communicate the enterprise values.

Policies need to be effective, efficient and non-intrusive. Non-intrusive is a specialist term that means that anyone who is expected to comply with a policy understands the reasoning in the policy and therefore is unlikely to resist conformance to a policy. It is important to ensure policies are readily available to stakeholders.

Frameworks need to be open, comprehensive and flexible such that changes to the enterprise's situation can be readily dealt with. The frameworks should be current in that they deal with the current governance direction and objectives. They also need to be available to all stakeholders.

Lifecycle:

Policies have a lifecycle and need a strong policy framework. This is vital to ensure that, for example, regulatory compliance by internal controls is met. A policy framework enables policy documentation to be structured into groupings and categories that make it easier for employees to find and understand the contents of policies. Policy frameworks can also be used to help in the planning and development of the policies for an organisation.

Good Practices:

As already stated, principles should be brief and simple.

Policies need to be explained in terms of their scope and validity and they should be revised regularly. It is vital to ensure mechanisms for the checking and measuring of compliance with policies are in place and that exceptions to policies can be handled using defined consequences for any stakeholder failing to obey policies; otherwise it is pointless having policies. Policies also need to meet the enterprise's risk appetite. A good source of policy statements is governance and management frameworks such as COBIT 5.

Enabler 2: Processes

Processes – meaning the 37 processes of COBIT 5 – is the most important enabler in most people's view. However, it is vital to recognise that implementing processes alone will not be totally effective. Other enablers are certainly needed as well – particularly the Culture, Ethics and Behaviour enabler that is needed to recognise why processes should be run and how they should be dealt with to manage and govern the enterprise. There have been many published examples over the past 20 years of enterprises formally introducing processes (e.g. ITIL and PRINCE2/PMBOK®) without ensuring culture changes are also put in place, and as a consequence the processes have not been highly effective at improving the running of the enterprise. In addition, the People, Skills and Competencies enabler is vital for ensuring process owners, managers and practitioners have the necessary ability to deal with processes.

COBIT 5 defines a process as 'a collection of practices influenced by the enterprise's policies and procedures that takes inputs from a number of sources (including other processes), manipulates the inputs and produces outputs (e.g. products and services).' This is a common style of definition for a process, although it is interesting to note that, in detail, inside each COBIT 5 process, it is specifically the management and governance practices of each process that accept the inputs and deliver the outputs (*see Figure 5.1*).

There are 37 COBIT processes and these are summarised in the Process Reference Model (*see Appendix B*).

Key Points

Stakeholders

Stakeholders are internal and external and cover a wide range of roles. Specifically, COBIT 5 processes each provide a RACI chart for 26 roles split into business and technology (*Table 5.5*).

Table 5.5: Process Stakeholders

Business	IT
Board	CIO
CEO	Head Architect
CFO	Head Development
COO	Head IT Operations
Business Executives	Head IT Administration
Business Process Owners	Service Manager
Strategy Executive Committee	Information Security Manager
Steering (Programme/Projects) Committee	Business Continuity Manager
Project Management Office	Privacy Officer
Value Management Office	
Chief Risk Officer	
Chief Information Security Officer	
Architecture Board	
Enterprise Risk Committee	
Head Human Resources	
Compliance	
Audit	

Goals

Each process in the *COBIT 5: Enabling Processes* manual describes process goals with metrics that enable measurement of the achievement of goals. However, under the ISO/IEC 15504 Information Technology: Process Assessment Standard that COBIT 5 uses for process assessment, the formal COBIT 5 Process Reference Model (PRM) has to use the terminology 'outcomes' instead of 'process goals'. Therefore, although the *COBIT 5: Enabling Processes* manual provides 'process goals and metrics' for each process, the PRM used for process assessment (in the *COBIT 5: Process Assessment Model (PAM): Using COBIT 5* manual) refers to these as 'outcomes'. They are word-for-word identical.

Process Goals are enabler goals and are, therefore, part of the COBIT 5 Goals Cascade (*see Chapter 4*).

Process goals should be intrinsic in that they conform to good practice – in particular, they are accurate and comply with internal and external rules. Processes should always be adopted and adapted as required to meet the enterprise's needs so that they are relevant and understandable; meaning they can be readily applied in the enterprise – that is, they meet contextual goals. If required, processes may be made confidential with controlled access – that is, they meet accessibility and security goals.

Lifecycle

To define, operate, monitor and optimise processes all steps of the generic Lifecycle should be used (*see Table 5.3*).

Good Practices

COBIT 5 processes are based on established best practices as discussed in *Chapter 2*.

Processes are arranged in domains and each process consists of practices with inputs and outputs. The details of a practice are defined as activities (*Figure 5.1*). The terminology used here is that used in the *COBIT 5: Enabling Processes* manual.

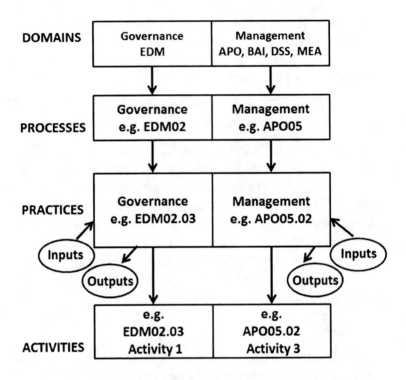

Figure 5.1: COBIT®5 Process Structure

Enabler 3: Organisational Structures

This enabler is quite simplistic and describes key factors to take into account when structuring organisational units that relate to all levels of governance and management activities.

Key Points

Stakeholders

Internal and external stakeholders may be used and they have various roles that include decision making, influencing and advising that relates to clients, suppliers, risks, audits and so on.

Goals

The goals for organisational structures are to have well-defined operating principles linked to other good practices that are mandatory for the enterprise to adopt.

Lifecycle

Organisational structures need to be planned, designed and created, operated, optimised and eventually disbanded when no longer required.

Good Practices

The good practices needed here are well established across most enterprises already, but to summarise they are:

- The operating principles, particularly staffing roles, frequency of meetings and documentation.
- The composition in terms of internal and external stakeholders that make up each organisational structural unit.
- Where decisions can be made in parts of the organisation – that is, how many staff are controlled by a manager. The term used by COBIT 5 is 'span of control'.

- Across which parts of the enterprise including processes does a person have control? The term used by COBIT 5 is 'level of authority/decision rights'.
- Permitted delegation of activities – that is, delegation of authority.
- The escalation structure and procedures for dealing with issues raised that can't be resolved normally. The term used by COBIT 5 is 'escalation procedures'.

Enabler 4: Culture, Ethics and Behaviour

Key Points

Stakeholders

Particular stakeholders for this enabler are those responsible for defining, implementing and enforcing desired behaviours in terms of rules and norms. Roles include: HR managers, risk managers, compliance managers, legal staff, and boards and panels such as promotion boards and remuneration and awards panels.

Goals

Goals are concerned with:

- Organisational ethics based on the desired enterprise values expressed in its principles.
- Personal ethics based on a person's life and feelings: for example, social background, religion, ethnicity, where they live, views they have adopted (e.g. green environment, human rights) or are forced to adopt

based on their role (e.g. a membership organisation's professional ethics)[72].

- Individual behaviours that include ethics collectively make up the enterprise's culture. Individual behaviours encompass personal ambitions, but interpersonal relations and willingness to obey enterprise policies are equally important. Particularly important behaviours relate to the enterprise's appetite for risk and the way the enterprise deals with negative outcomes. Clearly, good practice is to learn from negative outcomes and make improvements rather than blaming individuals for their behaviour.

Lifecycle

Lifecycles are needed to introduce good practices for culture, ethics and behaviour. The key activities needed are listed under good practices.

Good practices

Recognised good practices that assist the introduction and ongoing adoption of desired culture, ethics and behaviour include:

- Regular communication throughout the enterprise to encourage stakeholders to keep in place the desired behaviours and fully recognise corporate values.
- Raising awareness of desired behaviours by the exemplary behaviours demonstrated by senior managers and champions (both IT and business people).

---

[72] For example: ISACA® members' code of professional ethics. — *check it out*

- Encouragement of desired behaviours by the use of incentives and deterrents. Incentives include HR reward schemes. Deterrents will be the fact that contracts of employment or engagement formally state expected behaviours and staff are, therefore, aware of the consequences of disobedience such as verbal or written warnings leading to loss of employment or cessation of contracts.
- Rules and norms that are detailed guidance on behaviours to ensure adherence to policies.

Enabler 5: Information

It is well recognised in the modern world of computer-based information and knowledge that computers store data (just a bit pattern meaning, for example, the number 621) which is transformed and understood as information (e.g. the hotel room number you have been allocated). Information is transformed into knowledge from the experience of the use of information by many people (e.g. that a room with number 621 is likely to be on the 6th floor of a hotel, which may be unsuitable for someone with a fear of heights). It is business processes that use IT processes to generate and process data, which can then be transformed into information and knowledge.

Key Points

Stakeholders

All stakeholders are involved with information: information producers create information while information custodians store and maintain information. Others, called information consumers, only use information.

Goals

[handwritten: is this something to put in my spreadsheet?]

- **Intrinsic quality** of information is the amount of conformance with values. Is the information accurate (correct and reliable), objective (unbiased), believable (true and credible) and reputable (source is genuine or content is sound)?
- **Contextual quality** of information is its applicability and relevance to the user's tasks in that it is clearly and intelligibly presented. Key terms that COBIT 5 uses to describe the contextual quality of information are: relevancy, completeness, currency, appropriate amounts of information, concise and consistent representation, interpretability, understandability and ease of manipulation. Here is an example to show what these terms mean. Information is your personal credit card statement. It needs to be relevant in that it is for your company credit card only, not for all the staff in your company with company credit cards. It is complete in that it includes all transactions and it is current in that it covers only the past month. It will have appropriate amounts of information so you can identify the date, amount and company that the transactions were with. The statement will be concise and consistent in that it fits on just one or two pages and the format is the same every month and is always in your language and currency so that you can interpret and understand the meanings and amounts of transactions. Ease of manipulation would mean the included figures in the statement made it clear what the monthly automated or mandatory payment amount would be and the date that it will happen, as well as the remaining amount with the date that needed to be paid

[handwritten: does it have something similar]

to avoid interest and the amount of interest charged if the remaining amount is not paid by that date.

- **Security and accessibility** means information is available or obtainable when required and can be rapidly and readily retrieved. Access is restricted to authorised parties.

Lifecycle

The generic lifecycle applies as usual.

Important points to recognise are:

- Plan is the phase where information architectures and standards such as data definitions are prepared.

- Build/Acquire includes purchasing and access to external data sources as well as the creation of data records.

- Use/Operate includes store, share and use. Store is the phase where information is held in electronic form as files, databases or data warehouses, in hardcopy form or even in human memory! Share is the phase in which information is distributed and includes e-mailing messages, providing a website or a fileserver and so on. Use is the phase where information is used. Obvious examples include: raising alert messages as pop-ups on a screen and/or as e-mail messages; updating of real-time statistics such as departure and arrival times of airline flights; and converting dollars into euros when changing money at a bank.

Best practice

As discussed in *Chapter 2*, ISACA put in place an information model to deal with the significant increase in information and the need not only to manage information but also to select appropriate information to make effective business decisions. COBIT 5 therefore uses information systems theory (a major growth area in the past decade) and employs the well-established Semiotic Framework, which COBIT 5 uses as part of the COBIT 5 Information Model.

Here is a discussion of the background and origin to this theory.

Semiotics

A popular definition of semiotics is 'the study of signs' and it is concerned with the creation, representation and interpretation of signs. John Locke in 1690 stated that physics, ethics and semiotics were the three branches of human knowledge.

So what has a sign to do with information? Well, as de Saussure said in 1916: 'A sign consists of a signifier which is the form a sign takes and a signified which is the concept it represents.' (For example, © is the form of a sign for the concept of copyright.) Stamper[73] said that 'all information is carried or represented by signs.' For example, a network data packet is a sign, as is a business case document and a JavaScript™ program. So, signs consist of the form information takes and the concept it represents.

Why do information systems need to use signs? Stamper, in 1973, recognised that descriptions of information are 'extremely fuzzy' and a simple logical system is needed if information is to be carefully defined

---

[73] Stamper, R. K. (1973), *Information in Business and Administrative Systems*, London, Batsford.

using standard technical terms so that a scientific approach to the creation and development of information systems theory could be established. He realised that he could extend Morris' (1938) basic semiotic model to completely cover all levels of information. Let's first of all look briefly at Morris' semiotic model of signs.

Morris' Semiotic Model

Morris' semiotic model of signs had three levels:

- *Syntactics*, that is, structure
- *Semantics*, that is, meaning
- *Pragmatics*, that is, usage

This is the case for any sign. For example, © is the structure, copyright is the meaning and the usage is to place it on the colophon page (frontispiece) of a published book to remind readers about the copyright laws that apply.

Semiotics Framework (or Semiotics Ladder)

Here is a diagram (*Figure 5.2*) based on Stamper's Semiotic Ladder.

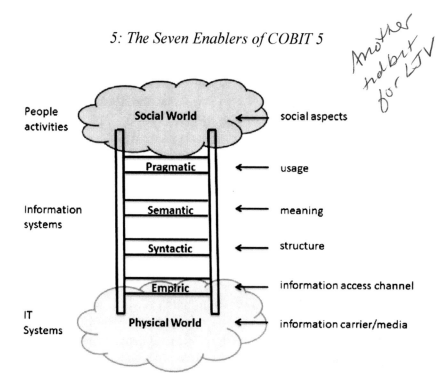

Figure 5.2: Semiotic Ladder. (After Beynon-Davies (2009)[74] and Stamper (1996)[75].)

Stamper recognised he needed to add Empiric and Physical levels so that information theory introduced by Shannon[76] in 1948 was incorporated, that is, the physics of signs that is the hardware used to transmit, receive and process them and the empirics of signs which covers patterns, variety, noise, channel capacity, codes and so on. The ladder from

---

[74] Beynon-Davies, P. (2009), *Business Information Systems,* Basingstoke, Palgrave Macmillan.

[75] Stamper, R. (1996) 'Signs, information, norms and systems' in *Signs of Work: Semiosis and Information Processing in Organisations,* (Ed. Holmquist, B., et al.), Berlin, de Gruyter.

[76] Shannon, C.E. (1948), 'A Mathematical Theory of Communication', *The Bell Systems Technical Journal, 27,* pp. 379–423, 623–656. Available at *http://cm.bell-labs.com/cm/ms/what/shannonday/shannon1948.pdf* (Accessed 5 September 2013).

Physical World to Social World covers data (Empiric and Syntactic) and information (Semantic and Pragmatic) that becomes knowledge in the Social World. The Physical World is where everything that can be empirically observed takes place. Information structures at the Pragmatic level is used to construct Social World activities such as creation and agreement of contracts, interpretation of a business case or management decision making based on balanced scorecard reports.

Examples of the layers are:

Physical world: Radio wave signals (Wi-Fi), square wave voltages on Ethernet cables, writing on paper or even 9000BC rock carvings at Cave of the Beasts, Wadi Sura in the Western Desert in Egypt.

Empiric: Wi-Fi channels, user interfaces.

Syntactic: Grammar rules such as subject verb object – for example, *the dog jumped the fence*, or programming language structures, for example, *IF (X .GT. 5) GO TO 100*[77].

Semantic: The meaning of information. For example, what does '*stone*' mean? Google and other search engines just think it means those five letters and finds everything including archaeological websites about Stonehenge, geological websites about rocks as well as websites about the rock groups The Rolling Stones and The Stone Roses! The semantic web, researched and developed by Tim

---

[77] A FORTRAN program statement.

Berners-Lee, the inventor of the World Wide Web, organises information by the meaning of *stone*. The semantic web approach is beginning to be used by search engines such as Google Knowledge Graphs, which searches for actual information about the subject of your query rather than just a list of links. Try typing Madonna into Google to see the Google Knowledge Graph result on the right-hand side of the page. COBIT 5 sees the meanings of the semantic layer as information type (e.g. personal or public), information currency (i.e. past, present or future) and information level (e.g. the different structure of daily, weekly and monthly reports from a Service Desk).

Pragmatic: The use of information that covers the structures and rules to be used. An example would be the format of a business case document with standardised headings and content together with the format that includes the date, author and version page at the front. COBIT 5 specifies: retention period, information status (e.g. current or historical), novelty (is it creative information or confirmation of existing information) and contingency (other information that this information needs as its source).

Social World: Is where information is used. Obvious examples of formal information are courts of law and religious services, but the presentation by physicists at CERN of experimental results in the search for the Higgs Boson needed to use very formal statistical graphs of their experimental results to convince the audience the results confirmed the presence of the Higgs Boson. The structure of the wall on your Facebook page is a Social World too, but it is not normally a key social world for enterprises using COBIT 5!

Enabler 6: Services, Infrastructure and Applications

IT services deliver outcomes to businesses. IT services are constructed of infrastructure and applications. Infrastructure is hardware (e.g. servers, routers, desktops, laptops, cables etc.), operating systems and facilities (buildings and power, air conditioning etc. for data centres). COBIT 5 uses the term service capabilities to mean the combination of services, infrastructure and applications.

Key Points

Stakeholders

Stakeholders deliver and use services. Delivery of services will be conducted by internal and external stakeholders since, in addition to an internal IT department, suppliers of some sort are always used (e.g. telcos, and operating system suppliers). In the case where extensive outsourcing is used there will still be internal stakeholders who manage the suppliers (e.g. the CIO and a small team). Users will be internal business users and external clients, partners and suppliers.

Goals

Goals that need to be met are provision of infrastructure and applications to create and run services. Services require an understanding of stakeholder needs in order to define service levels in service level agreements (SLAs) and deliver these.

Lifecycle

The Plan and Design steps of the lifecycle are where a target architecture is planned and designed for future services, infrastructure and applications. Architectures move from baseline architecture (i.e. existing architecture) via transition architectures (if needed) to target architecture. Transition architectures will be used when the timeframe for target architecture is long and intermediate stages are required.

Good practices

Enterprise architecture is the good practice and it provides overall guidance (via architecture principles) for governance of all implementation and use of IT-related resources.

Key enterprise architecture principles:

- The enterprise architecture should be as simple as possible yet must meet the enterprise's requirements, and that also means it must be agile to meet the changing needs of the enterprise.
- The enterprise architecture should use open industry standards, for example, TOGAF®, CEAF or FEA (*see Chapter 2*) for the enterprise architecture and ITIL for IT service management.
- Ensure components of the architecture can be reused when transition or target architectures are being designed.
- Purchase IT solutions rather than building an enterprise's own IT solutions in circumstances where that is possible and enterprise policies grant external purchase permission. Since enterprises' requirements in the modern era are changing regularly and new applications and hardware are constantly emerging

from suppliers, it is less effort to purchase rather than update or rewrite internal applications.

Enabler 7: People, Skills and Competencies

Clearly, to deliver any of the other enablers an enterprise needs people with appropriate skills and competencies.

Key Points

Stakeholders

Both internal and external people are stakeholders and every role will have a need for specific skills and competencies.

Goals

In this enabler, goals are the required skills and competencies together with the need to have required numbers of people and a desirable turnover rate – that is, not too high.

Lifecycle

The generic lifecycle applies to this enabler, of course, but the key parts are to understand the levels of skills required for roles and the numbers of people for each role. To meet the required skill levels people will need to be trained and/or skilled people recruited or suppliers used to conduct the roles. Periodically, it is essential to re-evaluate the required skills and competencies and this leads to training, external recruitment or use of appropriately skilled providers. As years go by some skills and competencies are no longer required and so people who do not have the desire to transform their skills will need to be made redundant. *—ugh!, I always want to transform my skills!*

Good practices

Required good practices are to define the roles in terms of skills and competencies and that is often conducted by the creation of formal job descriptions. However, a more detailed understanding of IT skills levels can be expressed in terms of skills categories (e.g. as required by 1st, 2nd and 3rd-line incident management practitioners). This has been particularly well expressed by the Skills Framework for the Information Age (SFIA[78]), initially created in 2003 and continually updated, currently at SFIA 5. The SFIA Foundation, the owner of SFIA, states that 'SFIA defines 96 professional IT skills, organised in six categories, each of which has several subcategories. It also defines seven levels of attainment, each of which is described in generic, non-technical terms.'

---

[78] *www.sfia-online.org/v501/en/publications/reference-guide/at_download/file.pdf.*

CHAPTER 6: DOMAINS AND PROCESSES

'If you can't describe what you are doing as a process, you don't know what you're doing.'

William Edwards Deming (1900-1993)

COBIT 5 has 37 processes in five domains. The governance domain: Evaluate, Direct and Monitor (EDM), has five processes, and the four management domains: Align, Plan and Organise (APO); Build, Acquire and Implement (BAI); Deliver, Service and Support (DSS); and Monitor, Evaluate and Assess (MEA), have the remaining 32 processes. *Table 6.1* shows how many processes there are in each domain and illustrates the main role of the domain.

Table 6.1: COBIT®5 Domains

Domain	Domain Name	Domain's main role	No. of processes
EDM	Evaluate, Direct and Monitor	Governance	5
APO	Align, Plan and Organise	Strategic	13
BAI	Build, Acquire and Implement	Tactical	10
DSS	Deliver, Service and Support	Operational	6
MEA	Monitor, Evaluate and Assess	Reporting	3
	Total		**37**

This chapter looks at the structure of processes as described in the *COBIT 5: Enabling Processes* guide. Remember what was discussed in <u>*Chapter 5*</u> (Enabler 2: Processes) that the structure of this guide is sometimes referred to as the Process Reference Model (PRM), but strictly speaking the formal Process Reference Model (PRM) – that is, a document that uses the formal terminology required by ISO/IEC 15504 – is only in the *COBIT 5: Process Assessment Model (PAM): Using COBIT 5*.

<u>*Appendix A*</u> lists all of the 37 processes and shows related frameworks and standards.

Each COBIT 5 process is structured in a consistent format that is extremely easy to understand and use. Each process is about four to six A4 pages. We are going to discuss the topics in the order in which they are described in each process. We will draw on two example processes:

- A governance process: EDM01: Ensure Governance Framework Setting and Maintenance.
- A management process DSS02: Manage Service Requests and Incidents.

Bold headings and italic fonts are word-for-word extracts from the *COBIT 5: Enabling Processes* guide.

An Example of a Governance Process

Process Number: *EDM01*
Process Name: *Ensure Governance Framework Setting and Maintenance*

Area: *Governance*
Domain: *Evaluate, Direct and Monitor*

Process Description: *Analyse and articulate the governance of enterprise IT, and put in place and maintain* *effective enabling structures, principles, processes and practices, with clarity of responsibilities and authority to achieve the enterprise's mission goals and objectives.*

Process Purpose Statement: *Provide a consistent approach integrated and aligned with the enterprise governance approach. To ensure that IT-related decisions are made in line with the enterprises' strategies and objectives, ensure the IT-related processes are overseen effectively and transparently, compliance with legal and regulatory requirements is confirmed and the governance requirements for board members are met.*

IT-related Goals: Appropriate IT-related goals (three) from the list of 17 IT-related goals discussed as part of the goals cascade in *Chapter 4*.

Related Metrics: Three or four metrics for measuring achievement of each IT-related goal.

Process Goals: Called process goals (three), but effectively these are the process outcomes.
desired ?
Related Metrics: Two or three metrics for measuring achievement of each process goal.

RACI Chart: The governance practices are defined (three) and numbered using decimal points:

EDM01.01   *Evaluate the governance system*
EDM01.02   *Direct the governance system*
EDM01.03   *Monitor the governance system.*

A RACI chart is provided that shows for each of these governance practices which of the 26 roles (*shown in Table 5.5 in Chapter 5*) are responsible, accountable, consulted or informed. Only one role is accountable for each governance practice.

Governance Practices, Inputs/Outputs and Activities:

Each of the governance practices *EDM01.01, EDM01.02* and *EDM01.03* is described with a brief paragraph explaining each governance practice. Each governance practice shows its inputs and its outputs. Inputs are frequently from other governance practices or management practices, but sometimes inputs are from *Outside COBIT*, for example, *regulations* for governance practice *EDM01.01* and *audit reports* for governance practice *EDM01.02*. Outputs are typically to other governance practices or management practices, for example, governance practice *EDM01.01* has an output *Authority levels* that is delivered to *All EDM* and to management practices *APO01.01* and *APO01.03*. Each governance practice also details the activities that make up the practice and these are a sentence each. For example, the governance practice *EDM01.01* has eight activities and the second one of these activities is *'Determine the significance of IT and its role with respect to the business.'*

Related Guidance: Describes related standards and/or frameworks with detailed reference to which section of a standard document or a specific framework guide is relevant. For example, the *Organisation for Economic Co-operation and Development (OECD)* has *Corporate Governance Principles* that can exist with the detailed definition of governance process *EDM01*.

6: Domains and Processes

An Example of a Management Process

Process Number: *DSS02*
Process Name: *Manage Service Requests and Incidents*

Area: *Management*
Domain: *Deliver, Service and Support*

Process Description: *Provide timely and effective response to user requests and resolution of all types of incidents. Restore normal service, record and fulfil user requests; and record, investigate, diagnose, escalate and resolve incidents.*

Process Purpose Statement: *Achieve increased productivity and minimise disruptions through quick resolutions of user queries and incidents.*

IT-related Goals: Appropriate IT-related goals (two) from the list of 17 IT-related goals discussed as part of the goals cascade in *Chapter 4*.

Related Metrics: Three or four metrics for measuring achievement of each IT-related goal.

Process Goals: Called process goals (three), but effectively these are the process outcomes.

Related Metrics: One or two metrics for measuring achievement of each process goal.

RACI Chart: The management practices are defined (seven) and numbered using decimal points:
DSS02.01   Define incident and service request classification schemes

DSS02.02	Record, classify and prioritise requests and incidents
DSS02.03	Verify, approve and fulfil service requests
DSS02.04	Investigate, diagnose and allocate incidents
DSS02.05	Resolve and recover from incidents
DSS02.06	Close service requests and incidents
DSS02.07	Track status and produce reports

A table is provided that shows for each of these management practices which of the 26 roles (*shown in Table 5.5 in Chapter 5*) are responsible, accountable, consulted or informed. Only one role is accountable for each management practice.

Management Practices, Inputs/Outputs and Activities:

Each of the management practices *DSS02.01, DSS02.02, DS02.03, DSS02.04, DSS02.05, DSS02.06* and *DSS02.07* is described with a brief paragraph explaining each management practice. Each management practice shows its inputs and its outputs. Inputs are frequently from other management practices or governance practices, but for the DSS02 management practices these are only from other management practices. Outputs are typically to other management practices or governance practices, but for all DSS02 processes its management practices are only linked to other management practices, for example, management practice *DSS02.04* has an output *Problem log* that is to management practice *DSS03.01*. Each management practice also details the activities that make up the practice and these are a sentence each. For example, the management practice *DSS02.05* has four activities and the third one of these activities is *Perform recovery actions if required.*

Related Guidance: Describes related standards and/or frameworks with detailed reference to which section of a standard document or a specific framework guide is relevant. For example, *ITIL V3 2011* is the related framework and the relevant sections are: *Service Operations, 4.2 Incident Management* and *Service Operation, 4.3 Request Fulfilment.*

CHAPTER 7: IMPLEMENTATION OF GEIT WITH COBIT 5

'The value of an idea lies in the using of it.'

Thomas Alva Edison
(1847-1931)

This chapter looks into the approach to implementation of Governance of Enterprise IT (GEIT) based on COBIT 5.

It is important to recognise there is not a mandatory approach to the implementation of GEIT – but the COBIT 5 books do provide sound guidance on approaches to consider, as well as discussion of difficulties that may arise and methods of avoiding or overcoming these. The key point to recognise is that governance and management of enterprise IT must be specific to your enterprise and that means analysis must be conducted with stakeholders, a business case must be devised, approval gained from senior management and an implementation programme devised and executed. Further, COBIT 5 is not the sole good practice as is well recognised by ISACA, despite the labelling of COBIT 5 as 'the only business framework for GEIT,' COBIT 5 is not only based on more than 80 other frameworks and standards as discussed in *Chapter 2* but also some of these frameworks, standards and good practices may already be in place and the enterprise needs to build on these. Common examples of good practices already in place in many enterprises today are ITIL, ISO20000, PRINCE2 or PMBOK®, ISO27001 and ISO9001.

Guidance on the implementation of GEIT using COBIT 5 is provided by ISACA in an outline in Chapter 7 of the book *COBIT 5: A Business Framework for the Governance and Management of Enterprise IT*. Detailed guidance is provided in the *COBIT 5: Implementation* guide.

Understanding the Enterprise

Many readers of this book are likely to have been employed in their enterprise for many years and so will have a strong understanding of their operations. Consultants who visit enterprises to assist with GEIT implementation will initially conduct activities to understand the enterprise. Areas to understand are:

Key areas

- Mission, vision and values (*aka* principles): already formally defined in most enterprises.
- Governance policies and practices: usually many of these already exist.
- Ethics and culture: not always formally defined but in many enterprises most staff already are aware of corporate ethics and certainly have personal ethics.
- Business strategy and plans: usually formally defined but periodically these are transformed to meet PESTLE[79] changes. Another key change factor that motivates strategic change is competitor products or services already in place or being developed.

---

[79] Politics, the economy, social changes, technology changes, legal changes and the emerging need to obey statutory environmental controls coupled with a desire to 'save the planet'.

- Risk appetite: often understood, but not always formally defined. Changes to risk appetite occur for specific key projects – for example, more risk may be taken in developing a new product or service but a capped budget is used to contain the risk[80].
- Industry practices: specifics that relate to the industry sector such as robotics in car production and highly sophisticated computer-based information systems now required in the car itself.
- Regulatory and statutory requirements: a constantly growing set of requirements including Data Protection legislation, Health and Safety legislation, Waste Electrical and Electronic Equipment (WEEE) directive (2002), Sarbanes-Oxley Act (2002), Basel II and III, Solvency II and Corporate Governance Codes.

Other important areas

- Operating model and level of maturity: the business processes that are dependent on people, processes and

---

[80] An interesting example of risk appetite many of you will be familiar with is Red Bull acting as the sponsor for the Red Bull Stratos project (2013) for Felix Baumgartner's skydive to the surface of the Earth from 39km (24 miles) into space. Red Bull sees itself as a company supporting and participating in extreme sports such as Formula 1 (motor racing) that align well with its energy drink. Although Project Stratos was a big risk, from Red Bull's viewpoint it fitted its brand and certainly gained international publicity (eight million viewers), and some financial pundits say it has already raised tens of millions of dollars from global exposure of its brand and it was the most money-earning marketing stunt ever. However, the project, which ran for seven years, had a constrained budgetary limit, initially $1M, but this was greatly extended to address technical difficulties with equipment design and according to some media articles was about $50M in total.

technology and how well these are currently operating from internal or external assessments.

- Capabilities and available resources: skills, expertise, experience and sufficient numbers of people to structure, organise and run the business and adequate resources such as facilities and equipment to operate successfully and, of course, budgets to fund everything.

Factors for successful implementation

It is extremely important to gain the support of Board members or top management because without their desire to have governance of enterprise IT in place, coupled with their commitment to support the implementation programme, then it is unlikely to be truly successful. In addition, key stakeholders need to support the GEIT programme too.[81] The programme to deliver GEIT needs to be communicated regularly to all types of audience to motivate people to adopt the desired changes. Building on existing good practices is vital to move to implementing the required enablers of COBIT 5 to deliver GEIT that fits the nature and desires of your enterprise. As with any programme, it is vital to implement quick wins, that is, relatively easy initiatives that can be implemented quickly in an attempt to secure support, fend off concerns at delays and also communicate success that will encourage participation in subsequent implementation stages.

---

[81] Take care not to select key stakeholders who only want to be on an e-mail distribution list so they know what is happening rather than they have a commitment to participate regularly in programme activities and are keen to allocate their staff to assist, too. Gain opinions from others about proposed key stakeholders – not easy to achieve without upsetting people and losing support, however.

Important factors that assist with gaining the support and commitment of board members, top managers and key stakeholders are to understand the pain points and triggers. Pain points are difficulties the enterprise is experiencing that are impacting its ability to successfully meet its business outcomes. Triggers are important changes that are taking place or need to take place. *Table 7.1* lists examples of key pain points and triggers. Appendix A of *COBIT 5: Implementation* provides mapping of pain points to COBIT 5 processes, giving guidance on processes that are likely to be important to implement to overcome the pain points. For example, the pain point 'Outsourcing service delivery problems' may be overcome by implementation of EDM04 Ensure Resource Optimisation, APO09 Manage Service Agreements and APO10 Manage Quality.

Table 7.1: Pain Points and Triggers to Assist Implementation of GEIT

Pain Points
Business frustration over failed IT initiatives, rising costs, low business value and return on investment (ROI)
Outsourcing service delivery problems
Duplicate projects
Continuous poor audit results
Board & senior managers reluctant to engage with IT
Triggers
Mergers, acquisitions or divestitures

Table 7.1: Pain Points and Triggers to Assist Implementation of GEIT cont.

Triggers continued.
New regulatory compliance requirements
Shift in market demand for company's products
Significant technology change
Mergers, acquisitions or divestitures

Another important approach to take into account when implementing COBIT 5 is to use the COBIT 5 Goals Cascade (*see Chapter 4*) to link stakeholder needs to business goals to IT-related goals to COBIT 5 processes and hence identify key processes to implement.

In addition, risk scenarios can be used to identify key COBIT 5 processes that can assist with risk management. Appendix C of *COBIT 5: Implementation* tabulates three key areas of risk:

- benefit/value enablement risk
- programme/project delivery risk
- service delivery/IT operation risk.

And each area identifies many risks such as:

- incorrect technology selection in terms of cost, performance features and compatibility
- insufficient quality of project deliverables
- intrusion of malware on critical operational servers and/or laptops.

It then shows against each risk the COBIT processes that are capable of assistance. For example, the risk of intrusion of malware on critical operational servers and/or laptops can be controlled with the COBIT 5 processes:

- APO01 Manage the IT Management Framework (using management practice APO01.08 Maintain compliance with policies and procedures).
- DSS05 Manage Security Services (using management practice DSS05.01 Protect against malware).

Lifecycle Approach to Implementation

Experts in the field of governance of enterprise IT have worked on how to use COBIT to implement IT governance since before 2003, the era of COBIT 3, when ISACA first published its *IT Governance Implementation Guide*. There have been three completely new editions of ISACA guides to GEIT implementation as ISACA introduced new versions of COBIT and other frameworks such as Val IT™. Experience of best practice grew as implementations were conducted and expertise grew. The current edition, *COBIT 5: Implementation,* is based on a lifecycle approach of seven phases that is neatly presented as a radar-style diagram (*Figure 7.1*).

The seven phases of the lifecycle are based on the approach used by Kotter (1996)[82] for the implementation of change known as his '8 steps for transformation'. Kotter's approach is also used for ITIL implementation, although ITIL does not include the broad range of concepts that COBIT 5 has adopted.

---

[82] Kotter, J. P. (1996), *Leading Change*, Boston, Harvard Business School Press.

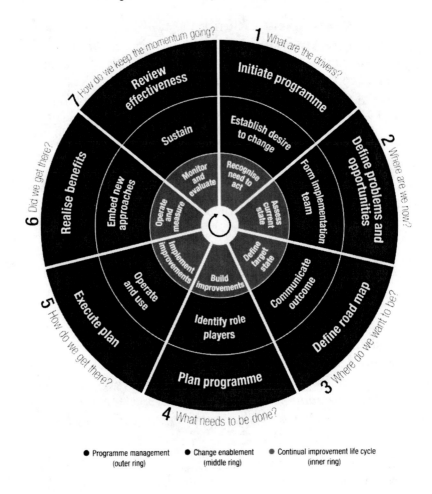

- Programme management (outer ring)
- Change enablement (middle ring)
- Continual improvement life cycle (inner ring)

Figure 7.1: Lifecycle for Implementation of IT Governance Using COBIT®5 (© 2012 ISACA®)

The seven phases are listed in _Table 7.2._

Table 7.2: Phases of the COBIT®5 Implementation Lifecycle

Implementation Phases	
1	What are the drivers?
2	Where are we now?
3	Where do we want to be?
4	What needs to be done?
5	How do we get there?
6	Did we get there?
7	How do we keep the momentum going?

[handwritten: Perhaps also as implement change model - for future reference]

Each implementation phase requires three separate but linked areas of activity to be covered together; shown as concentric bands of separate colours in *Figure 7.1*. These are:

- Programme management – a programme of projects
- Change enablement – cultural and behavioural changes needed
- Continual improvement lifecycle – details of improvement activities.

All three of these activities must be collectively conducted in each lifecycle phase as shown in *Table 7.3*.

Table 7.3: Relationship Between Activities that Should Take Place Within Each Phase

	COBIT 5 Implementation Lifecycle						
	Phase						
	1	2	3	4	5	6	7
	What are the drivers?	Where are we now?	Where do we want to be?	What needs to be done?	How do we get there?	Did we get there?	How do we keep the momentum going?
Programme Management (PM)	Initiate programme	Define problems & opportunities	Define road map	Plan programme	Execute plan	Realise benefits	Review Effectiveness
Change Enablement (CE)	Establish desire to change	Form implementation team	Communicate outcome	Identify role players	Operate and use	Embed new approaches	Sustain
Continual Improvement Lifecycle (CI)	Recognise need to act	Assess current state	Define target state	Build improvements	Implement improvements	Operate and measure	Monitor and evaluate

It is important to recognise that continual improvement happens throughout the implementation lifecycle; not solely after the implementation has been completed.

Each phase of the lifecycle is formally explained in detail in Chapter 6 of *COBIT 5: Implementation* in terms of the following areas:

- Phase objective and description
- Many tasks: separately listed for PM, CE and CI
- Inputs and outputs.

For each phase of the lifecycle, roles and responsibilities need to be allocated to staff covering the activities of programme management (PM), change enablement (CE) and continual improvement CI. Chapter 6 of the *COBIT 5: Implementation* guide provides a RACI chart for each lifecycle phase with detailed descriptions of roles and responsibilities for each activity conducted. A summary of these roles and responsibilities is provided in *Table 7.4*.

Table 7.4: Roles and Responsibilities in Implementation Lifecycle Phases

Roles	Phases of Implementation Lifecycle						
	1	2	3	4	5	6	7
Board	C/I	I	I		I	I	C/I
IT Executive Committee	A/R	A/C/I	A/I	A/I	A/I	A/I	A/I
CIO	R	R	R	R/C	R/C	A/R/C	A/R/C
Business Executive	R/C	R/C	R/C	R/C/I	R/C/I	R/C	R/C
IT Managers	C/I	R/C	R/C	R/C	R	R/C	R/C
IT Process Owners	C/I	R/C	R/C/I	R/C	R/C	R/C	R/C
IT Audit	C/I	C	C/I	C/I	C/I	C/I	R/C
Risk and Compliance	C/I	R/C	C/I	C/I	C/I	C/I	C/I
Programme Steering	R	A/R	A/R	A/R	A/R	R/I	R/I

A = Accountable   R = Responsible   C = Consulted   I = Informed

Notes:

Board does not have a role in Phase 4, although some Boards may expect information.

Only a single role should be accountable for an activity in a phase.

Several activities take place in each phase, which is why more than a single role has A.

The other key requirements in the implementation lifecycle are to recognise that in each phase there are several challenges to overcome such as:

Phase 1: Lack of senior management buy-in, commitment and support.

Phases 2 & 3: Cost of improvements outweighing perceived benefits.

Phase 4: Resistance to change.

Phase 5: Trying to do too much at once; tackling overly complex and/or difficult problems.

Phases 6 & 7: Difficulty in showing or proving benefits.

The guide, *COBIT 5: Implementation* (Chapter 4), tabulates 21 challenges in total and with each challenge provides many causes coupled with recognised advice on techniques to use to overcome each challenge.

Finally, one of the key parts of the Implementation Lifecycle Phase 2: Where are we now? is assessment of the current state, a CI activity. A key part of this assessment is to determine the 'as-is' state, particularly of key COBIT 5 processes that the enterprise has decided are needed to implement GEIT. Then the gap between the 'as-is' state and the 'to-be' state can be determined to plan the implementation activities. Assessment of processes has been conducted in earlier versions of COBIT using CMM® or CMMI® (*see Chapter 2*). However, in COBIT 5, this has been switched to using the international standard ISO/IEC 15504 Software Engineering – Process Assessment Model and this and the method of using it is discussed in the next chapter.

CHAPTER 8: COBIT 5 PROCESS ASSESSMENT MODEL (PAM)

'Measurement is the first step that leads to control and eventually to improvement. If you can't measure something, you can't understand it. If you can't understand it, you can't control it. If you can't control it, you can't improve it.'

H. James Harrington

This chapter discusses the approach to process assessment. As discussed in <u>*Chapter 7*</u> this is needed in Phase 2 of the implementation lifecycle to implement GEIT but is also regularly used to assess the state of COBIT 5 processes with the goal of recognising process improvements needed or to gain confirmation about the current status of COBIT 5 processes.

Traditionally, COBIT has used a maturity model based on CMMI® as its technique of assessing processes. However, with the introduction of COBIT 5 this has changed and now the standard COBIT approach to assessment is to use the COBIT 5: Process Assessment Model (PAM) that is conformant with ISO/IEC 15504-2 Software Engineering – Process Assessment: Performing an Assessment. Now the terminology used is 'capability assessment based on a process capability model' rather than 'maturity assessment using a maturity model'.

COBIT 5 Process Assessment Model

The COBIT 5 Process Assessment Model (PAM) is shown in *Figure 8.1*.

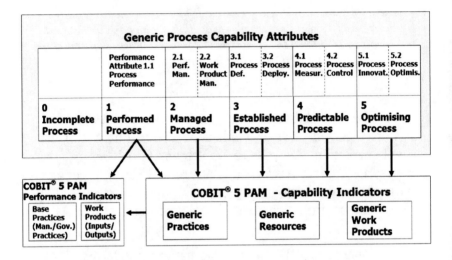

Figure 8.1: COBIT®5 Process Assessment Model (PAM)[83]

(This figure is derived from Figure 19, p.42 of *COBIT 5: A business framework for the governance and management of enterprise IT).*

The PAM model has to completely obey the rules set out in the ISO/IEC 15504 international Standard. This means there must be a Process Reference Model (PRM)

---

[83] People often ask me 'why is there an arrow linking Level 1 Performed Process to The COBIT®5 PAM – Capability Indicators when Level 1 does not use Generic Practices and Generic Work Products, only Levels 2–5 use those.' It is absolutely true that Levels 2–5 use Generic Practices and Generic Work Products, but according to ISO/IEC 15504 Generic Practices can be used to aid the audit of Base Practices. COBIT®5 documentation contradicts its diagram and does state that 'only Levels 2-5 assessment use Generic Practices and Generic Work Products.'

formulated using ISO/IEC 15504 terminology. As already discussed in *Chapter 6*, the formal COBIT 5 Process Reference Model conformant with ISO/IEC 15504 terminology is in *COBIT 5: Process Assessment Model (PAM): Using COBIT 5.* It is recommended that to fully understand this difference in terminology, you should spend 10 minutes comparing a process in the *COBIT 5 Enabling Processes* book with the *COBIT 5: Process Assessment Model (PAM): Using COBIT 5.* This will make it absolutely clear what terminology is being used to conduct assessment. If conducting a self-assessment then you can manage without viewing the PAM book, but it is better to use it, I would suggest.

How assessment is conducted

There are six capability levels 0–5 and these are listed in *Table 8.1*, which shows the name of each capability level. Levels are assessed using process attributes. Apart from Level 1, each capability level has two process attributes that must both be assessed for that capability level.

Assessment of Level 1 uses only base practices, that is, practices that belong to the process being assessed. Failing to meet Level 1 means the process is at Level 0 Incomplete.

Levels 2–5 use only generic practices that are identical for every COBIT process. However, each process attribute has different generic practices. Generic practices are described in *COBIT 5: Self-assessment Guide: Using COBIT 5* as well as in the *PAM* guide, but generic work products are not described in the *COBIT 5: Self-assessment Guide: Using COBIT 5* book but are only in the *PAM* guide. Finally, note that in *Figure 8.1*, the Generic Resources shown in the COBIT 5 Process Assessment Model – Capability

Indicators are formally a part of ISO/IEC 15504 but have not been used as part of the COBIT 5 Process Assessment Model.[84]

---

[84] Generic Resources has been shown on *Figure 8.1* to be consistent with diagrams used in COBIT®5 books, but it was not defined as part of COBIT®5 as it is not essential.

Table 8.1: COBIT®5 Capability Levels, Process Attributes, Practices and Work Products Used for Assessment

Capability Level	Level Name	Process Attributes		Practices and Work Products used for Assessment	
0	Incomplete				
1	Performed	PA1.1	Process Performance	Base Practices	Work Products[1]
2	Managed	PA2.1	Performance Management	Generic Practices	Generic Work Products
		PA2.2	Work Product Management	Generic Practices	Generic Work Products
3	Established	PA3.1	Process Definition	Generic Practices	Generic Work Products
		PA3.2	Process Deployment	Generic Practices	Generic Work Products
4	Predictable	PA4.1	Process Measurement	Generic Practices	Generic Work Products
		PA4.2	Process Control	Generic Practices	Generic Work Products
5	Optimising	PA5.1	Process Innovation	Generic Practices	Generic Work Products
		PA5.2	Process Optimisation	Generic Practices	Generic Work Products

[1] Work Products are helpful for assessing Base Practices, but for Self-Assessment they do not have to be used

Assessment of a Process Attribute uses an ISO/IEC 15504 rating scale. The rating scales are labelled as N, P, L, F and are shown in *Table 8.2*, which is based upon ISO/IEC 15504-2: 2003:

Table 8.2: COBIT®5 PAM Rating Scales

Rating	Rating Name	Achievement percentage
N	Not achieved	0 – 15
P	Partially achieved	>15 – 50
L	Largely achieved	>50 – 85
F	Fully Achieved	>85 – 100

Level 1 Assessment

What is being assessed for a process is, 'Are Process Outcomes being achieved?'

Process Outcomes are listed in the *PAM* guide and are shown with labels such as DSS02-01, which are assessed by Base Practices labelled for example as DSS02-BP1. Work Products are labelled for example as DSS02-WP1. Note that the Process Outcomes are what the *COBIT 5 Enabling Processes* book labels as Process Goals (with numbers 1, 2, 3 and so on) and it labels Base Practices as Management Practices[85] labelled for example as DSS02.01

---

[85] Since DSS02 is a Management Process not a Governance Process.

(i.e. with decimal point). It labels as Inputs and Outputs what the *PAM* guide calls Work Products.

Level 2–5 Assessments

What is being assessed for a process is, 'Are Generic Practices being achieved?'

Generic Practices (GP) are different for each process attribute (PA) but are identical for every process. The *PAM* guide labels Generic Practices, for example for Capability Level 2, as:

- Level 2 PA2.1 as GP 2.1.1, GP 2.1.2, GP 2.1.3, GP 2.1.4, GP 2.1.5, GP 2.1.6
- Level 2 PA2.2 as GP 2.2.1, GP 2.2.2, GP 2.2.3, GP 2.2.4

Generic Work Products (GWP) are a set of values that are applied differently to each Capability Level. This is tabulated clearly in section 4.0 of the *PAM* guide. The Generic Work Products are labelled as:

- GWP 1.0, GWP 2.0, GWP 3.0, GWP 4.0, GWP 5.0, GWP 6.0, GWP 7.0, GWP 8.0, GWP 9.0

Generic Work Products that are listed in the table in *PAM* guide section 4.0 against a Generic Practice are used to assist the assessment of Generic Practices.

There are strict rules about how assessment at different Capability Levels can be evaluated:

- Essentially to meet a Capability Level then L or F as the Rating Scale must be achieved.

- For Capability Levels 2–5 both PAs must be at Rating Scale L or F and all Capability Levels below that level must be at Rating Scale F.

Table 8.3 demonstrates these rules to show what Rating Scales are needed for Process A to be at Capability Level 1, Process B to be at Capability Level 2 and Process 3 to be at Capability Level 3.

	Level 1	Level 2		Level 3	
Process	**PA 1.1**	**PA 2.1**	**PA 2.2**	**PA 3.1**	**PA 3.2**
A	L or F				
B	F	L or F	L or F		
C	F	F	F	L or F	L or F

Table 8.3 Demonstration of Rules for Attainment of a Capability Level

Advantages of the Process Assessment Model (PAM) scheme

Unlike the traditional CMMI®-based scheme that COBIT used in the past, this COBIT 5 PAM scheme is reliable and repeatable because specific practices (Base Practices and Generic Practices) and specific work products (Work Products and Generic Work Products) have been defined. This means assessors have much detail to formally examine when making their assessments. With the old scheme, the approach to conducting assessment was not rigorously defined and so different assessors did assessment in different ways.

Further, assessment is conducted according to an international standard and it is worth noting that ISO20000 is currently working to develop assessment using ISO15504, too.

CHAPTER 9: COBIT 5 RESOURCES

'You cannot open a book without learning something.'

Confucius (551-479 BC)

This chapter discusses the official COBIT 5 documentation and the official COBIT 5 training courses and certifications.

Documentation

ISACA's COBIT documentation has a reputation for being state of the art and highly accurate. The COBIT 5 framework was developed by an international team of experts and the draft design (April 2010) and subsequent draft documents (July 2011) were both publicly published as exposure drafts for worldwide public reviews and then revised and peer-reviewed before formal documentation was published in April 2012[86] and is listed in *Table 9.1.*

Apart from the overview document that may be considered a Framework document since that is its title: *COBIT®5: A Framework for the Governance and Management of Enterprise IT*, the other COBIT 5 documentation is divided into two main categories: Enabler and Professional. Enabler documents provide detailed information about a specific enabler: initially published was Enabling Processes, then in late 2013 Enabling Information will be published and perhaps later other enablers? Professional documents relate to roles: implementation, assessment, assurance, risk management, information security.

---

[86] *www.ISACA.org/cobit/pages/faqs.aspx.*

Professional documents may later be published for other roles such as IT service management.

All documentation is available as printed books or downloadable PDF files. Most documentation is freely available to ISACA members, but some books are only available to ISACA members by purchase.

Since COBIT 3, COBIT has also provided an online database that contains key COBIT documentation and provides a discussion forum and a benchmarking database. This is still under development for COBIT 5 at the time of writing this book (September 2013) and a tentative release in late 2013 has been announced that will provide access to COBIT 5 publications. Other non-COBIT, ISACA content and other GEIT content is tentatively planned to be available in early 2014. In addition, in mid-2014, further growth will provide the ability to customise COBIT to fit enterprise needs and to provide multi-user access, too.

Table 9.1 COBIT®5 Resources

Guide type	Title	Publication Date	Pages
Framework	COBIT®5: A Business Framework… Free download from www.isaca.org/COBIT	April 2012	94
Enabler	COBIT®5: Enabling Processes	April 2012	230
Enabler	COBIT®5: Enabling Information	Nov 2013	
Professional	COBIT®5: Implementation	April 2012	78
Professional	COBIT®5 for Information Security	July 2012	219
Professional	COBIT®5 for Assurance (?)	May 2013	318
Professional	COBIT®5 for Risk	Oct 2013	216
Professional	COBIT® 5 Assessment Programme *COBIT® 5 Process Assessment Model: Using COBIT® 5* *COBIT® 5 Assessor Guide: Using COBIT® 5 and Tool Kit* *COBIT®5 Self-assessment Guide: Using COBIT® 5 and Tool Kit*	Jan 2013	144 52 24
Professional	COBIT®5 Online	~ Q4 2013	

Training and Certification

COBIT 5 training is controlled and run by APMG in conjunction with ISACA. APMG/ISACA jointly organise the syllabi for COBIT 5 courses and set and mark exams. In addition APMG/ISACA assesses training organisations and appoints them as accredited training organisations (ATOs) for COBIT 5. Trainers working for COBIT 5 ATOs must have appropriate background and experience relating to the COBIT 5 courses they teach and they must themselves have passed exams with 67 percent compared to the pass mark of 50 percent.

There are three COBIT 5 courses with a roadmap for training shown in *Figure 9.1*.

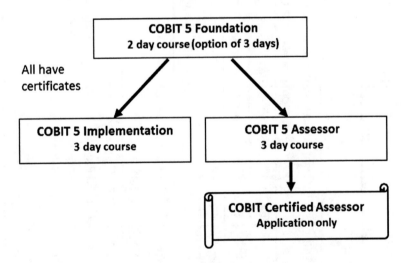

Figure 9.1: Roadmap of COBIT®5 Certifications

Each course has a multiple-choice exam in the final hours of the course that leads to gaining a certificate if the 50 percent pass mark is reached. Exam style and duration are shown in _Table 9.2:_

Table 9.2 Examinations for COBIT®5 Certifications

Exam	Type	No. of Questions	Duration
COBIT®5 Foundation	Multi-choice: single correct answer	50	40 minutes
COBIT®5 Implementation	Case-study based multi-choice with variable question types	4 Each question has multiple parts	2 hours 30 minutes
COBIT®5 Assessor	Case-study-based multi-choice with variable question types	4 Each question has multiple parts	2 hours 30 minutes

The exams on the COBIT 5 Implementation and COBIT 5 Assessor courses can only be taken by candidates who already hold a COBIT 5 Foundation Certificate and who have attended official training courses run by ATOs.

The COBIT Certified Assessor is not a training course but a certificate granted to professionals who hold both COBIT® Foundation and COBIT 5 Assessor Certificates and can provide documented evidence of work experience in the field of business management, IT management or management consultancy. Two years' experience can be substituted by holding a Certified Information Systems

Auditor (CISA®) Certificate or other relevant auditing or assessment qualifications. To maintain possession of a COBIT Certified Assessor Certificate two assessments must be conducted every two years.

APPENDIX A: COBIT 5 PROCESSES AND OTHER FRAMEWORKS AND STANDARDS USED

COBIT® Process No.	COBIT® Process Name	Related Guidance Frameworks and Standards
EDM01	Ensure Governance Framework Setting and Maintenance	COSO, ISO/IEC 38500, King III, OECD
EDM02	Ensure Benefits Delivery	COSO, ISO/IEC 38500, King III
EDM03	Ensure Risk Optimisation	COSO/ERM, ISO/IEC 31000, ISO/IEC 38500, King III
EDM04	Ensure Resource Optimisation	ISO/IEC 38500, King III, TOGAF® 9
EDM05	Ensure Stakeholder Transparency	COSO, ISO/IEC 38500, King III
APO01	Manage the IT Management Framework	ISO/IEC 20000, ISO/IEC 27002
APO02	Manage Strategy	ITIL 2011
APO03	Manage Enterprise Architecture	TOGAF® 9
APO04	Manage Innovation	*None*
APO05	Manage Portfolio	ISO/IEC 20000, ITIL 2011, SFIA
APO06	Manage Budget and Costs	ISO/IEC 20000, ITIL 2011
APO07	Manage Human Resources	ISO27002, SFIA

Appendix A

COBIT® Process No.	COBIT® Process Name	Related Guidance Frameworks and Standards
APO08	Manage Relationships	ISO/IEC 20000, ITIL 2011
APO09	Manage Service Agreements	ISO/IEC 20000, ITIL 2011
APO10	Manage Suppliers	ISO/IEC 20000, ITIL 2011, PMBOK®
APO11	Manage Quality	ISO 9001:2008
APO12	Manage Risk	ISO27001:2005, ISO/IEC 27002:2011, ISO/IEC 31000
APO13	Manage Security	ISO/IEC 27001:2005, ISO27002:2011, NIST SP800-53 Rev 1
BAI01	Manage Programmes and Projects	PMBOK®, PRINCE2
BAI02	Manage Requirements Definitions	ITIL 2011
BAI03	Manage Solutions Identification and Build	*None*
BAI04	Manage Availability and Capacity	ISO/IEC 20000, ITIL 2011
BAI05	Manage Organisational Change Enablement	Kotter (1996), *Leading Change,* Boston, Harvard Business School Press
BAI06	Manage Changes	ISO/IEC 20000, ITIL 2011
BAI07	Manage Change Acceptance and Transitioning	ISO/IEC 20000, ITIL 2011, PMBOK®, PRINCE2
BAI08	Manage Knowledge	ITIL 2011
BAI09	Manage Assets	ITIL 2011

COBIT® Process No.	COBIT® Process Name	Related Guidance Frameworks and Standards
BAI10	Manage Configuration	ISO/IEC 20000, ITIL 2011
DSS01	Manage Operations	ITIL 2011
DSS02	Manage Service Requests and Incidents	ISO/IEC 20000, ISO27002, ITIL 2011
DSS03	Manage Problems	ISO/IEC 20000, ITIL 2011
DSS04	Manage Continuity	BS 25999-2007 (now ISO22301:2012), ISO/IEC 27002:2011, ITIL 2011
DSS05	Manage Security Services	ISO/IEC 27002:2011, NIST SP800-53 Rev 1, ITIL 2011
DSS06	Manage Business Process Controls	*None*
MEA01	Monitor, Evaluate and Assess Performance and Conformance	ISO/IEC 20000, ITIL 2011
MEA02	Monitor, Evaluate and Assess the System of Internal Controls	*None*
MEA03	Monitor, Evaluate and Assess Compliance with External Requirements	*None*

APPENDIX B: COBIT 5: PROCESS REFERENCE MODEL

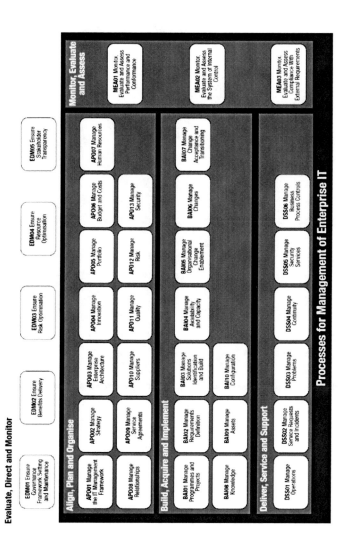

Figure B.1: COBIT® 5 Process Reference Model (© 2012 ISACA®)

APPENDIX C: COBIT 5 GOALS CASCADE

Table C.1: Stakeholder Needs mapped to Enterprise Goals (© 2012 ISACA®)

STAKEHOLDER NEEDS	1. Stakeholder value of business investments	2. Portfolio of competitive products and services	3. Managed business risk (safeguarding of assets)	4. Compliance with external laws and regulations	5. Financial transparency	6. Customer-oriented service culture	7. Business service continuity and availability	8. Agile responses to a changing business environment	9. Information-based strategic decision making	10. Optimisation of service delivery costs	11. Optimisation of business process functionality	12. Optimisation of business process costs	13. Managed business change programmes	14. Operational and staff productivity	15. Compliance with internal policies	16. Skilled and motivated people	17. Product and business innovation culture
How do I get value from the use of IT? Are end users satisfied with the quality of the IT service?	X	X					X					X	X			X	X
How do I manage performance of IT?					X	X				X				X			
How can I best exploit new technology for new strategic opportunities?	X	X						X					X			X	X

Table C.1 Stakeholder Needs mapped to Enterprise Goals - continued

STAKEHOLDER NEEDS	1. Stakeholder value of business investments	2. Portfolio of competitive products and services	3. Managed business risk (safeguarding of assets)	4. Compliance with external laws and regulations	5. Financial transparency	6. Customer-oriented service culture	7. Business service continuity and availability	8. Agile responses to a changing business environment	9. Information-based strategic decision making	10. Optimisation of service delivery costs	11. Optimisation of business process functionality	12. Optimisation of business process costs	13. Managed business change programmes	14. Operational and staff productivity	15. Compliance with internal policies	16. Skilled and motivated people	17. Product and business innovation culture
How do I best build and structure my IT department?								■		■	■	■		■	■	■	
How dependent am I on external providers? How well are IT outsourcing agreements being managed? How do I obtain assurance over external providers?			■	■					■	■							
What are the (control) requirements for information?			■						■						■		
Did I address all IT-related risk?			■				■										

Table C.1 Stakeholder Needs mapped to Enterprise Goals - continued

STAKEHOLDER NEEDS	1. Stakeholder value of business investments	2. Portfolio of competitive products and services	3. Managed business risk (safeguarding of assets)	4. Compliance with external laws and regulations	5. Financial transparency	6. Customer-oriented service culture	7. Business service continuity and availability	8. Agile responses to a changing business environment	9. Information-based strategic decision making	10. Optimisation of service delivery costs	11. Optimisation of business process functionality	12. Optimisation of business process costs	13. Managed business change programmes	14. Operational and staff productivity	15. Compliance with internal policies	16. Skilled and motivated people	17. Product and business innovation culture
Am I running an efficient and resilient IT operation?					■		■										
How do I control the cost of IT? How do I use IT resources in the most effective and efficient manner? What are the most effective and efficient sourcing options?										■	■	■	■	■			
Do I have enough people for IT? How do I develop and maintain their skills, and how do I manage their performance?										■	■	■	■	■			
How do I get assurance over IT?				■											■		

Table C.1 Stakeholder Needs mapped to Enterprise Goals (© 2012 ISACA®)

STAKEHOLDER NEEDS	1. Stakeholder value of business investments	2. Portfolio of competitive products and services	3. Managed business risk (safeguarding of assets)	4. Compliance with external laws and regulations	5. Financial transparency	6. Customer-oriented service culture	7. Business service continuity and availability	8. Agile responses to a changing business environment	9. Information-based strategic decision making	10. Optimisation of service delivery costs	11. Optimisation of business process functionality	12. Optimisation of business process costs	13. Managed business change programmes	14. Operational and staff productivity	15. Compliance with internal policies	16. Skilled and motivated people	17. Product and business innovation culture
Is the information I am processing well secured?				■			■								■		
How do I improve business agility through a more flexible IT environment?	■							■								■	■
Do IT projects fail to deliver what they promised—and if so, why? Is IT standing in the way of executing the business strategy?		■	■								■	■	■				

144

Appendix C

Table C.1 Stakeholder Needs mapped to Enterprise Goals – continued

STAKEHOLDER NEEDS	1. Stakeholder value of business investments	2. Portfolio of competitive products and services	3. Managed business risk (safeguarding of assets)	4. Compliance with external laws and regulations	5. Financial transparency	6. Customer-oriented service culture	7. Business service continuity and availability	8. Agile responses to a changing business environment	9. Information-based strategic decision making	10. Optimisation of service delivery costs	11. Optimisation of business process functionality	12. Optimisation of business process costs	13. Managed business change programmes	14. Operational and staff productivity	15. Compliance with internal policies	16. Skilled and motivated people	17. Product and business innovation culture
How critical is IT to sustaining the enterprise? What do I do if IT is not available?		■					■										
What concrete vital primary business processes are dependent on IT, and what are the requirements of business processes?											■	■					
What has been the average overrun of the IT operational budgets? How often and how much do IT projects go over budget?					■					■	■			■			

Appendix C

Table C.1 Stakeholder Needs mapped to Enterprise Goals – continued

STAKEHOLDER NEEDS	1. Stakeholder value of business investments	2. Portfolio of competitive products and services	3. Managed business risk (safeguarding of assets)	4. Compliance with external laws and regulations	5. Financial transparency	6. Customer-oriented service culture	7. Business service continuity and availability	8. Agile responses to a changing business environment	9. Information-based strategic decision making	10. Optimisation of service delivery costs	11. Optimisation of business process functionality	12. Optimisation of business process costs	13. Managed business change programmes	14. Operational and staff productivity	15. Compliance with internal policies	16. Skilled and motivated people	17. Product and business innovation culture
How much of the IT effort goes to fighting fires rather than to enabling business improvements?		X	X									X					
Are sufficient IT resources and infrastructure available to meet required enterprise strategic objectives?		X			X					X							
How long does it take to make major IT decisions?	X			X	X			X									
Are the total IT effort and investments transparent?				X	X												
Does IT support the enterprise in complying with regulations and service levels? How do I know whether I am compliant with all applicable regulations?				X											X		

146

(handwritten note: "like a Balanced Score Card?")

Table C.2 Enterprise Goals mapped to IT-related goals (© 2012 ISACA®)

| | | Enterprise Goal | | | | | | | | | | | | | | | | |
| | | Financial | | | | | Customer | | | | | Internal | | | | | Learning and Growth | |
	IT-related Goal	1. Stakeholder value of business investments	2. Portfolio of competitive products and services	3. Managed business risk (safeguarding of assets)	4. Compliance with external laws and regulations	5. Financial transparency	6. Customer-oriented service culture	7. Business service continuity and availability	8. Agile responses to a changing business environment	9. Information-based strategic decision making	10. Optimisation of service delivery costs	11. Optimisation of business process functionality	12. Optimisation of business process costs	13. Managed business change programmes	14. Operational and staff productivity	15. Compliance with internal policies	16. Skilled and motivated people	17. Product and business innovation culture
01	Alignment of IT and business strategy	P	P	S			P		P	P	P	P	S	P			S	S
02	IT compliance and support for business compliance with external laws and regulations		S	S	P		S		S	P						P		
03	Commitment of executive management for making IT-related decisions	P	S				P		P	P				P				S
04	Managed IT-related business risk			P	S			P	S	S	P	S			S	S	S	
05	Realised benefits from IT-enabled investments and services portfolio	P	P				S	S	S	S		S	P	S	S		S	S
06	Transparency of IT costs, benefits and risk	S		S		P			S	S	P	S	P					
Financial																		

Table C.2 Enterprise Goals mapped to IT-related goals continued

		Enterprise Goal																	
			Financial					Customer					Internal					Learning and Growth	
	IT-related Goal		1. Stakeholder value of business investments	2. Portfolio of competitive products and services	3. Managed business risk (safeguarding of assets)	4. Compliance with external laws and regulations	5. Financial transparency	6. Customer-oriented service culture	7. Business service continuity and availability	8. Agile responses to a changing business environment	9. Information-based strategic decision making	10. Optimisation of service delivery costs	11. Optimisation of business process functionality	12. Optimisation of business process costs	13. Managed business change programmes	14. Operational and staff productivity	15. Compliance with internal policies	16. Skilled and motivated people	17. Product and business innovation culture
Customer	07	Delivery of IT services in line with business requirements	P	P	S	S		P	P	P	S		P	S	S			S	S
	08	Adequate use of applications, information and technology solutions	S	S	S	S		S	S		S	S	P	S	S	P		S	S

148

Table C.2 Enterprise Goals mapped to IT-related goals continued

		IT-related goal																	
Internal	09	IT agility	S	P		S					P		P		P	S		S	S	P
	10	Security of information, processing infrastructure and applications		P						P								P			
	11	Optimisation of IT assets, resources and capabilities	P	S							S		P	P	S	P				S	S
	12	Enablement and support of business processes by integrating applications and technology into business processes	S	P		S		S		S	S	P	S	S	S	S				S	S
	13	Delivery of programmes delivering benefits, on time, on budget, and meeting requirements and quality standards	P	S		S		S		S	S	S	S	P							
	14	Availability of reliable and useful information for decision making	S	S		S			P	S			P								
	15	IT compliance with internal policies		S		S			P	S							P				
Learning and Growth	16	Competent and motivated business and IT personnel	S	P	P	S		P	S	S	S		S					P		P	S
	17	Knowledge, expertise and initiatives for business innovation	P			S				P	S	P	S	S	S	S			S	P

Table C.3 IT-related Goals mapped to COBIT 5 Processes © 2012 ISACA®©

COBIT 5 Process	IT-related Goal																
	Financial					Customer			Internal							Learning and Growth	
	01	02	03	04	05	06	07	08	09	10	11	12	13	14	15	16	17
	Alignment of IT and business strategy	IT compliance and support for business compliance with external laws and regulations	Commitment of executive management for making IT-related decisions	Managed IT-related business risk	Realised benefits from IT-enabled investments and services portfolio	Transparency of IT costs, benefits and risk	Delivery of IT services in line with business requirements	Adequate use of applications, information and technology solutions	IT agility	Security of information, processing infrastructure and applications	Optimisation of IT assets, resources and capabilities	Enablement and support of business processes by integrating applications and technology into business processes	Delivery of programmes delivering benefits, on time, on budget, and meeting requirements and quality standards	Availability of reliable and useful information for decision making	IT compliance with internal policies	Competent and motivated business and IT personnel	Knowledge, expertise and initiatives for business innovation

Appendix C

Table C.3 IT-related Goals mapped to COBIT 5 Processes - continued

Evaluate, Direct and Monitor																		
EDM01	Ensure Governance Framework Setting and Maintenance	P	S	P	S	P	S	S	S	S	S		S	S	S	S	S	S	S
EDM02	Ensure Benefits Delivery	P	S	S	P	P	S	P	P	S	S	S	S	S	S	S	S	S	P
EDM03	Ensure Risk Optimisation	S	S	S	P	P	S	S	S	S	S	P	P	S		S	P	S	S
EDM04	Ensure Resource Optimisation	S	S	S	S	S	S	S	S	S	P	P	P		S			P	S
EDM05	Ensure Stakeholder Transparency	S	S	P		P	P										S	P	S

Table C.3 IT-related Goals mapped to COBIT 5 Processes - continued

COBIT 5 Process	IT-related Goal																
	Financial						**Customer**		**Internal**							**Learning and Growth**	
	01	02	03	04	05	06	07	08	09	10	11	12	13	14	15	16	17
	Alignment of IT and business strategy	IT compliance and support for business compliance with external laws and regulations	Commitment of executive management for making IT-related decisions	Managed IT-related business risk	Realised benefits from IT-enabled investments and services portfolio	Transparency of IT costs, benefits and risk	Delivery of IT services in line with business requirements	Adequate use of applications, information and technology solutions	IT agility	Security of information, processing infrastructure and applications	Optimisation of IT assets, resources and capabilities	Enablement and support of business processes by integrating applications and technology into business processes	Delivery of programmes delivering benefits, on time, on budget, and meeting requirements and quality standards	Availability of reliable and useful information for decision making	IT compliance with internal policies	Competent and motivated business and IT personnel	Knowledge, expertise and initiatives for business innovation

Table C.3 IT-related Goals mapped to COBIT 5 Processes - continued

Align, Plan and Organise	AP001	Manage the IT Management Framework	P	P	S	S	S	S	P	S	S	S	S	P	P	P			
	AP002	Manage Strategy	P		S	S	S	S	S	S	S	S	P	S	S	P			
	AP003	Manage Enterprise Architecture	P		S	S	S	S	P	S	P	S	S	P	S	S			
	AP004	Manage Innovation	S		S	P	P		P		P	S		P		P			
	AP005	Manage Portfolio	P		S	P	S	S	S	S	S	P	S		S	S			
	AP006	Manage Budget and Costs	S		S	P	S	P	S		S								
	AP007	Manage Human Resources	P	S	S	S	P	S	S		S	S	P	P	P	P		S	
	AP008	Manage Relationships	P		S	S	P	S	S	S	S	S		S	P	P		S	
	AP009	Manage Service Agreements	S		S	S	S	S	S	S	S	S	P	S	S	S		S	
	AP010	Manage Suppliers		S	P	S	P	S	P	S	S	S		S	P	S	P	S	
	AP011	Manage Quality	S	S	S	P	S	P	S	S				S	S	S	S	S	
	AP012	Manage Risk	P	P	P		P	S	P		P	P	S	P	P	P	S	S	
	AP013	Manage Security	P	P	P		P	P			P	P					S		P

Table C.3 IT-related Goals mapped to COBIT 5 Processes - continued

IT-related Goal		
Financial	01	Alignment of IT and business strategy
	02	IT compliance and support for business compliance with external laws and regulations
	03	Commitment of executive management for making IT-related decisions
	04	Managed IT-related business risk
	05	Realised benefits from IT-enabled investments and services portfolio
	06	Transparency of IT costs, benefits and risk
Customer	07	Delivery of IT services in line with business requirements
	08	Adequate use of applications, information and technology solutions
	09	IT agility
Internal	10	Security of information, processing infrastructure and applications
	11	Optimisation of IT assets, resources and capabilities
	12	Enablement and support of business processes by integrating applications and technology into business processes
	13	Delivery of programmes delivering benefits, on time, on budget, and meeting requirements and quality standards
	14	Availability of reliable and useful information for decision making
	15	IT compliance with internal policies
Learning and Growth	16	Competent and motivated business and IT personnel
	17	Knowledge, expertise and initiatives for business innovation
COBIT 5 Process		

Table C.3 IT-related Goals mapped to COBIT 5 Processes - continued

		1	2	3	4	5	6	7	8	9	10	11	12	13	14	15	16	17
Build, Acquire and Implement	BAI01 — Manage Programmes and Projects	S	S			P		S			S	S			S			P
	BAI02 — Manage Requirements Definition	S			S	S	P	S	S	S	S	P	P	S	S	S	S	P
	BAI03 — Manage Solutions Identification and Build	S			S	S	S	S			S	P	P	S	S			S
	BAI04 — Manage Availability and Capacity	S			P	S		P		S	S	P	P					
	BAI05 — Manage Organisational Change Enablement	P				P	S	S		S	P	S		S	S	S		S
	BAI06 — Manage Changes	S		S	S	S	S	S	P	S	S	P	P	S	S			
	BAI07 — Manage Change Acceptance and Transitioning	S		S	S	S	P			P	P	S	S	S	S			
	BAI08 — Manage Knowledge	P	S		S			S	S	S	S	S	S	S			S	S
	BAI09 — Manage Assets			S	S			P	S	S			P					S
	BAI10 — Manage Configuration			S	P			P	S	S	S		S			P	S	P

155

Table C.3 IT-related Goals mapped to COBIT 5 Processes - continued

COBIT 5 Process	IT-related Goal																
	Financial						Customer		Internal							Learning and Growth	
	01	02	03	04	05	06	07	08	09	10	11	12	13	14	15	16	17
	Alignment of IT and business strategy	IT compliance and support for business compliance with external laws and regulations	Commitment of executive management for making IT-related decisions	Managed IT-related business risk	Realised benefits from IT-enabled investments and services portfolio	Transparency of IT costs, benefits and risk	Delivery of IT services in line with business requirements	Adequate use of applications, information and technology solutions	IT agility	Security of information, processing infrastructure and applications	Optimisation of IT assets, resources and capabilities	Enablement and support of business processes by integrating applications and technology into business processes	Delivery of programmes delivering benefits, on time, on budget, and meeting requirements and quality standards	Availability of reliable and useful information for decision making	IT compliance with internal policies	Competent and motivated business and IT personnel	Knowledge, expertise and initiatives for business innovation

Appendix C

Table C.3 IT-related Goals mapped to COBIT 5 Processes - continued

	Process	1	2	3	4	5	6	7	8	9	10	11	12	13	14	15	16	17
Deliver, Service and Support	DSS01 Manage Operations		S		P	P		P	S	S	S	P			S	S	S	S
	DSS02 Manage Service Requests and Incidents				P	P		P	S	S	S				S	S		S
	DSS03 Manage Problems	S	S		P			P	S	S		P	S		P	S		S
	DSS04 Manage Continuity	S	S		P	S		P	S	S	S	S	S		P	S	S	S
	DSS05 Manage Security Services	P	P		P	S		S	S	P	P	S	S		S	S		
	DSS06 Manage Business Process Controls	S	S		P			P	S	S	S	S	S		S	S	S	S
Monitor, Evaluate and Assess	MEA01 Monitor, Evaluate and Assess Performance and Conformance	S	S	S	P	S	S	P	S	S	S	P		S	S	P	S	S
	MEA02 Monitor, Evaluate and Assess the System of Internal Control	P			P	S	S	S	S	S	S				S	P		S
	MEA03 Monitor, Evaluate and Assess Compliance With External Requirements	P			P	S	S	S	S	S					S	S		S

157

INDEX

I

implementation	105-117
lifecycle	111-117
information	
empiric	35-36, 89-90
model	35, 45, 86-87
physical world	35-36, 90
pragmatic	35-36, 88-91
security	24-26
semantic	35-36, 90-91
social world	35-36, 90-91
syntactic	35-36, 88, 90
innovation	45, 135
inputs	77, 79, 102, 115, 125
internal controls	32-33, 137
intrinsic quality	71, 85
ISACA	11, 12, 22, 24, 33
ISF	25
ISO31000	22-23
ISO9000 series	16, 29
ISO/IEC 15504 series	30-32, 78, 98, 120-124
ISO/IEC 20000 series	16-19
ISO/IEC 27000 series	24-26
ISO/IEC 38500 series	12-13, 43-44
IT governance	7-10, 12-13
IT Steering Committee	60
IT Strategy Committee	59-60
ITAF	45
ITGI	9, 43, 63, 64
ITIL	13-16, 34, 57, 77, 93, 103, 111

Index

Index

Index

ITG RESOURCES

IT Governance Ltd sources, creates and delivers products and services to meet the real-world, evolving IT governance needs of today's organisations, directors, managers and practitioners.

The ITG website (*www.itgovernance.co.uk*) is the international one-stop-shop for corporate and IT governance information, advice, guidance, books, tools, training and consultancy.

www.itgovernance.co.uk/cobit.aspx is the information page on our website for COBIT resources.

Other Websites

Books and tools published by IT Governance Publishing (ITGP) are available from all business booksellers and are also immediately available from the following websites:

www.itgovernance.eu is our euro-denominated website which ships from Benelux and has a growing range of books in European languages other than English.

www.itgovernanceusa.com is a US$-based website that delivers the full range of IT Governance products to North America, and ships from within the continental US.

www.itgovernanceasia.com provides a selected range of ITGP products specifically for customers in the Indian sub-continent.

www.itgovernance.asia delivers the full range of ITGP publications, serving countries across Asia Pacific. Shipping from Hong Kong, US dollars, Singapore dollars, Hong Kong dollars, New Zealand dollars and Thai baht are all accepted through the website.

Toolkits

ITG's unique range of toolkits includes the IT Governance Framework Toolkit, which contains all the tools and guidance that you will need in order to develop and implement an appropriate IT governance framework for your organisation.

For a free paper on how to use the proprietary Calder-Moir IT Governance Framework, and for a free trial version of the toolkit, see *www.itgovernance.co.uk/calder_moir.aspx*.

Training Services

IT Governance Ltd offers an extensive portfolio of training courses designed to educate information security, IT governance, risk management and compliance professionals. Our classroom and online training programmes will help you develop the skills required to deliver best practice and compliance to your organisation. They will also enhance your career by providing you with industry standard certifications and increased peer recognition. Our range of courses offer a structured learning path from Foundation to Advanced level in the key topics of information security, IT governance, business continuity and service management.

COBIT 5 is the internationally accepted best practice framework for effective IT governance and control. With a focus on managing processes, it has helped organisations throughout the world bridge the gaps between governance, control requirements, regulatory compliance and business risks. Knowledge and experience in implementing COBIT 5 are both essential to ensuring that business and IT objectives are fully aligned. COBIT 5 qualifications are also a key requirement for the career development of any IT governance professional.

> *Try to do a COBIT 5 Foundations Training Course*

At IT Governance, we offer a comprehensive programme of IT governance training including the COBIT 5 Foundation and COBIT 5 Implementation courses. Each course is designed to provide delegates with relevant knowledge and skills and an industry recognised qualification awarded by APMG International.

Full details of all IT Governance training courses can be found at *www.itgovernance.co.uk/training.aspx*.

Professional Services and Consultancy

We can help you to implement the COBIT 5 framework correctly from the outset. This is something that is virtually impossible to do 'out of the box' given the comprehensive nature of COBIT.

To ensure that you achieve your goals in the shortest possible time, draw upon the services of IT Governance. Our expert consultants have substantial experience of COBIT 5 and international management systems, which when brought together will help you get the best value out of COBIT controls.

When properly applied, COBIT 5 can address all of the relevant internal and external IT services, in addition to internal and external business processes. Using our unique approach, your risk and compliance (IT-GRC) practitioners can readily understand COBIT 5 and see how to drive implementation of GEIT using COBIT 5 and how process assessment is best conducted.

For more information about IT Governance Consultancy & Training Services for COBIT 5 see:

www.itgovernance.co.uk/consulting.aspx.

Publishing Services

IT Governance Publishing (ITGP) is the world's leading IT-GRC publishing imprint that is wholly owned by IT Governance Ltd.

With books and tools covering all IT governance, risk and compliance frameworks, we are the publisher of choice for authors and distributors alike, producing unique and practical publications of the highest quality, in the latest formats available, which readers will find invaluable.

www.itgovernancepublishing.co.uk is the website dedicated to ITGP enabling both current and future authors, distributors, readers and other interested parties, to have easier access to more information. This allows ITGP website visitors to keep up to date with the latest publications and news.

Newsletter

IT governance is one of the hottest topics in business today, not least because it is also the fastest moving.

You can stay up to date with the latest developments across the whole spectrum of IT governance subject matter, including; risk management, information security, ITIL and IT service management, project governance, compliance and so much more, by subscribing to ITG's core publications and topic alert emails.

Simply visit our subscription centre and select your preferences: *www.itgovernance.co.uk/newsletter.aspx*.